NUMEROLOGY REVEALS YOUR ALL

NUMEROLOGY REVEALS YOUR ALL

Your Personality
and Karmic Lessons
Within Your Birth Numbers

FRANK BUGGE

PRESIDING ARCHBISHOP OF THE AUSTRALIAN BRANCH
OF THE WORLDWIDE CATHOLIC APOSTOLIC CHURCH
OF ANTIOCH—MALABAR RITE

Blue Dolphin Publishing

Published by Blue Dolphin Publishing, Inc.
P.O. Box 8, Nevada City, CA 95959
Orders: 1-800-643-0765
Web: www.bluedolphinpublishing.com

ISBN: 978-1-57733-266-4 paperback
ISBN: 978-1-57733-435-4 e-book

Library of Congress Control Number: 2014935723

First Printing, March 2014

Printed in the United States of America

5   4   3   2   1

CONTENTS

FOREWORD

This system of numerology is for the purpose of primarily getting to know one's self and realizing the shortcomings of our own personality and thus endeavour to overcome them. It also helps to understand the other members of humanity that we come across, and are more able to understand their problems when counselling and advising. This is NOT for the use of exploiting anyone in any way, and any person attempting to use it for that purpose will be viewed with utter contempt.

This little book is especially for those who have tried to find a book on numerology that is accurate and instead found an enormous quantity of completely fanciful airy-fairy stuff that is in no way commensurate with facts of any living person or useful in any way whatsoever.

When practising numerology, do not be afraid to see, know and understand the negative aspects of the personality. Most people today have been conditioned to be aware of the negative rather than the positive, but it is essential to the well being of society and the individual that we emphasize the positivity of the Character, for in so doing we give the person the opportunity to use the character tools with a more constructive attitude. With this in mind let us remember the question asked in the Bible: Am I my Brother's Keeper??? Here the answer should be YES.

I base this numerology on over thirty years of using this art to counsel and understand those who are in need of help, and I have found this system to be of great value in my years of acting within the role of my clerical pathway. Like any other skill, do not for one moment think you shall gain the instant ability and use without some practice. To do anything well one must practice, but with very little effort you will soon see the results in this system, and you will improve with each time you read a birth date. You can learn to read the numbers in weeks, and after a few months you will amaze yourself at how easy this becomes. The accuracy of this system will never cease to astound you as your ability grows. Quite often I have had some of my pupils saying, "I found myself saying stuff that I have never yet worked out how I arrived at, and it was right." The amazing answer to this is that this system also develops your intuitive ability as you use it. By studying this system you shall also see how that is possible.

I must state that there are those who will scoff at this and approach this book in a negative way and/or doubt my sanity, but then again the hierarchy of the day scoffed at many people like Leonardo DaVinci, Galileo, Isaac Newton, Albert Einstein, Louis Pasteur, Christopher Columbus, Jesus, and so many others too numerous to name. If I can possibly merit the same scorn as these folk, I shall be indeed lifted to the heights of ecstasy and be happy that at least some one has taken notice of my literary adventure.

To illustrate what the advantage of numerology can be, I have had a very competent doctor learn and use this skill in trying to quickly gain an insight into the personality and the problems of certain patients. This gave the doctor a head start in understanding the patient, but like any good doctor she did not rely on this numerology without the backup of facts. Naturally I will not reveal this doctor's name for fear of her getting the wrath of the medical profession of using what they regard as a "QUACK" system. I can however assure you that she is very thorough in her diagnoses and also uses conventional means to back up any decision, but this knowledge of numerology certainly does give her a head start.

I have also taught this system to a professional counsellor who is employed by the juvenile counselling system, and she also uses this to great advantage and almost instantly gains the confidence of the people she is assisting. It is quite obvious that some folk are quickly at ease if they realize that you can understand their inner frustrations and feelings. This results in them being far more ready to accept your assistance when they see you have an insight as to where they are coming from.

True numerology is actually a short-cut system of Astrology in the main, but like the field of astrology, for every numerologist who is accurate and true in this subject, there are sadly many fakers who are out for a quick buck, and consequently deliver a load of garbage. These fakers simply tell the person what they would love to hear. This is NOT numerology, but a cheap form of fraud. The accuracy of the numerology system within this book will stand on its own merits and that is how I like it to be.

Numerology also points out that the medical mental experts do not always know the answers, and are very quick to throw accusations like schizophrenic, mentally incompetent, breakdown, unstable, highly strung, etc, when a person is actually Clairvoyant, intuitive or Clairaudient or just a restless person. This attitude results in shattering the person's confidence entirely, and these in-genuine members of the medical fraternity finish up destroying many lives in the process. I quote one case where this has happened to a teenager, and she was mentally bludgeoned and drugged into believing she was unstable. The simple truth was she had incredible clairvoyant and clairaudient abilities as was discovered just before she died in her late 60s. Nearly all those years of her life was lived under the influence of the drugs she was prescribed by the medical profession. While the medical profession acted in all good faith according to the limit of this particular doctor's knowledge (or lack thereof), it did not help the person one iota to overcome her problem of hearing voices, but had her living in a state of drugged misery and in the end she was convinced she was mad.

I acknowledge Bishop Chearle and Bishop Glenn Clark, who have both given of their time to check this book out and make sure it has circumvented any tendency for errors.

WHY DOES
NUMEROLOGY WORK

It is stated by great mathematicians that the whole Universe exists because of numbers. These great experts of the numbers include the sheer genius of the likes of Pythagoras, Euclid, Hypatia, J.S Bach, and Isaac Newton, just to name a few. These men and women were brilliant scientists as well as psychics. Even though they were psychics, they were certainly not inclined to fantasy, and could literally prove their statements.

Everything in creation has a resonant frequency that is responsible for keeping that substance in its natural form. This includes light, noise, solids of all sorts. Hark back to a few years ago and see why people like soldiers marching always had to break step when going over a small bridge. If they didn't, after a few minutes the bridge would collapse because the resonant frequency of marching soldiers was very close to the bridge's natural frequency.

Take the famous opera tenor Caruso, who could shatter glass at will by holding a certain note for a length of time. Another great singer who could do this was John McKormic, the wonderful Irish singer.

Each note has a certain vibration, and vibration is simply the number of cycles per second it moves.

Light is also vibration and differing light frequencies shine out as different colors to our eyes. Changing the light's frequencies (numbers of cycles) will change the color.

Let us look at water. If we heat it, it speeds up the number of cycles and therefore changes to steam when the speed has altered enough. If we cool it, it slows down the cycles and goes solid.

Science can prove that everything that appears solid is actually atoms bound together by their magnetic attraction generated by their frequency of vibration.

Look at the basic atom and you will see all the electrons whirling around the nucleus in a certain speed. Compare the atom with our Universe, and here we see that the Universe seems to be an atom on a much larger scale. Numbers of electrons then denote what material the atom is.

Our physical being only exists because we have a natural vibration in ourselves, hence the saying "I do or don't like this person's vibes." Such statements are perfectly true as we all differ slightly in our vibration rate. Dogs can sense this very well. If we decide to investigate our higher self, i.e. our spirit, we will find that our spiritual side is a much higher vibration than our physical side. We can call our spiritual side our Ghost, Spirit, etc. or whatever we like, but if we could slow down that spirit side like we slow down the vibration of water, then that spirit would become solid for a while until we relaxed and the Spirit would then resume its natural vibration. Of course such slowing of our psychic self would require enormous self-control and ability. This is actually how Jesus appeared and disappeared to his disciples when he was already dead. He was powerful enough to control his spirit and to do this at will. We of humanity have a long way to go to reach this state because it requires great purity of mind and body. Sadly the average present-day human is lacking here.

As native American Chief Seattle once said, "We do not own the Earth, it owns us and we are part of it." If this be so which it surely is, then it becomes obvious that if we have certain vibrations of numerical basis, then the Universe must also have the same basic numerical structure.

Because of the fact we can now see that numbers can and do change many things, let us look at our incarnations, and attempt to understand exactly how the numbers operate and literally control our personality.

BASICS FACTS OF NUMEROLOGY

Before we start going into the numbers themselves, we must understand some basic facts.

The birth date MUST be taken in standard time NOT daylight saving time or any such other time. If daylight saving time is in vogue at the place where the person was born, then it should be translated into normal standard time. This could make a difference of one day or the next if the person was born around midnight. Imagine a person born at 11:30 PM in standard time, but the place was using daylight saving time and therefore quoted 12:30 AM the next day. This would make the reading inaccurate and this must be avoided if one is to read the numbers properly. The Universe has decreed that normal time has midday with the sun centered directly at mid-point overhead, and at these times certain energies issuing forth from the planetary systems and stars suddenly change. Cosmic energies change promptly at these certain times settled upon by the universe, and our daylight saving system will not in the least change those solar times. Cosmic energies change at precisely 12 midnight, 6 AM, 12 noon, and 6 PM.

We humans, being the natural egotists that we are, have come to believe that there is the situation where a doctor thinks he or she has decided to bring on the birth of a baby, or perform a caesarean, and they think they have made this big decision of exactly when a child shall be born. Poor deluded Souls we humans are to think such a thing, for let me state here and now that the Soul of the entity that is being born has already taken this into account, and we mortals on the physical are miles behind any decision the Soul makes regarding its future incarnation. The entity being born has decided when and where it will be born, so that it will get the opportunity to learn the lessons that the Soul designates that it must physically learn in this incarnation. We mortals now, and will always in the future, simply fall into line with this decision of the Soul of the incarnating person.

Of course there are the sceptics who will now say, "If we know when and where we were to be born, we would not get born into places where life is miserable." This would be a gross inaccuracy, for that is precisely the lesson some people are to experience in their particular life. The spiritual entity demands that they learn this lesson for its advancement in evolution, and each of us MUST go through all these experiences eventually, including male, female, and even homosexual lifetimes, to be able to fully comprehend the full reason and system of life. Just imagine if we as children decided not to learn our mathematics because it was too hard or we did not like it. How would this affect us in later life when we could not do the simple basic Arithmetic? We would be in a really sad state. The spirit also learns lessons it does not like, but like the mathematics in our daily lives, they are necessary for our Soul's growth. It is truly said, experience is the best teacher, and the Soul knows this to be a fact. Whether you do or do not believe in this re-incarnation thing does not matter a fig to the Soul, for the results will still work out exactly the same, but it does help to understand why this works.

When an entity wishes to incarnate, its Soul will always visit the future parents it has chosen and request their permission to become the Soul's parents. This happens during the sleep time of the future parents and they are visited on the astral psychic level and this matter is discussed. This is an infallible rule and the parents always have free will if they wish to accept this or not. Very rarely will the requested parents refuse this. Of course we of humanity existing on the physical see things differently by only being capable of viewing a fraction of the picture, but the entity keeps their eye out in readiness for this opportunity to incarnate with the desired universal energies necessary for teaching the lessons the Soul wants to experience. The Soul is not concerned if the lessons are hard or not, but all the same it will never give out a lesson that is impossible to overcome and absorb by the physical body. That would destroy the purpose of the whole learning process and would be wasteful of an incarnation. The Soul also has to contend with the fact that it has to pay karma to other people they knew in past lives, so the parent is almost always someone they have had past lives with in one way or another, and Karma exists between them. You will therefore realize that the Soul is very careful when it chooses the parents for their next incarnation, and thus their karmic lessons.

For those who wish to know more about the psychic level that instigates and controls the birth time and date, I shall now show the levels that control the lessons learned by the entity, which is of course the Soul. We start by seeing the level of our being right from our highest level of existence. The Monadic level is our highest self and is the level where the Bible truly states "We are Created by God in His image." Our monad therefore sends us down to learn everything about the existence of Creation, but we must start at the bottom in all things to learn the basics: Monadic—Atmic—Nirvanic—Buddhic—Mental—Astral—Physical: see grid below for breakdown of these levels.

Monadic
Atmic
Nirvanic
Buddhic
Mental
Astral
Physical

It does not take any genius to know that we are normally at the physical level, which is the lowest level of existence. When we sleep however, our Soul allows ourselves to rise to the astral level.

Now each of these levels shown above, are divided into seven levels called sub-planes, and these sub-planes are again divided into seven levels called sub-sub planes. This applies to ALL the levels except one, and the one variation here is the Mental level which has a different divisional set-up. The mental division is divided up as shown in the following grid.

1st Sub-Plane	1 Sub-sub-plane upper mental		
2nd Sub-Plane	2 "	"	"
	3 "	"	"
	4 " ***	"	" Soul
3rd Sub-Plane	5 "	"	"
	6 "	"	"
	7 "	"	"
4th Sub Plane	1 Sub-sub-plane Lower mental		
5th Sub-Plane	2 "	"	"
	3 "	"	"
6th Sub-Plane	4 "	"	"
	5 "	"	"
7th Sub-Plane	6 "	"	"
	7 "	"	"

*** Indicates the level of your Soul which will always control the incarnation and lessons of the entity and therefore the birth time and date. This will apply to past and future incarnations, for the Soul has complete mastery when and where you will incarnate up until the time where you will not need to incarnate anymore. Contrary to popular belief of many people, the Soul is NOT the highest level of our existence or indeed anywhere near it, in fact it is less than half way up the scale.

Each grid division is a Sub-plane, and the right side of the grid are the sub-sub-planes within the sub-plane. You will notice that the Soul level is on the 2nd sub-plane and the fourth sub-sub-plane. This is the level that chooses when you will re-incarnate and under what Astral influences, and thus the date and time of your next birth. Whether you completely understand this or not will not affect your ability to read the numerology. It matters not if you completely disagree on this point, the readings will still be accurate.

THE RAYS

There are seven main rays in existence within the universe, and the entity decides to also be born under a particular ray as well as under the other selected energies of the universe. This is another careful manipulation of the birth-time by the entity to also fit into the correct rays system. This ray system changes every 13 days. The day and night system are complementary to each other and they change promptly at 6 AM and 6 PM in a split second. While in very advanced numerology these AM and PM times are taken into account, for normal reading this is not necessary and we shall not go into this here. These rays are always the same for any given date. An example of this is that January the first will always be Red AM Ray and Violet PM Ray. I know there will be a change within the leap year as some smart cookie is bound to point out. In a leap year the extra day in February puts all the rays one day behind, but they equal out on December the twenty-second and twenty-third in a leap year, and just the twenty-third on a non-leap year. The ancients believed that the 23rd of December was not part of the normal year and so began the saying of "a year and a day." On these two days in a leap year (22nd and 23rd) the rays are White daytime and Black night-time. On a non-leap year it is just the 23rd that is under the black and white ray. These rays NEVER occur on any other day. As you can now work out, the 13-day Ray system is always consistent.

The Ray energies are the result of the internal actions and reactions of forces generated between the spheres of the force Cosmos, the Force Chaos and the balancing force of the sphere known as the Ring Pass Not, and these three forces we know as the Divine God produced the Trinity of Creation.

The Ray system of the Red, Orange, Yellow, Green, Blue, Violet and Indigo Rays influence and condition us for thirteen days, each one coming to us in modified form after absorption, and being passed on by the Planets of the Solar System. This system also provides us with our birth Rays, arranged in pairs: Black and White, Red and Violet, Blue and Yellow, Green and Green, and Indigo and Orange.

For those interested to know which ray they were born on, the two charts are added in this book. For normal numerology this is not relevant unless you are going into advanced numerology which is not included in this book. You will note that the dates start on 24th December, which is actually the day the year starts in the Solar world.

The Black and White Rays only provide pathways for incarnations during the night and day on December 23rd on a non leap year, and 22nd and 23rd on a leap year. This is the one time of the year when all biorhythms are in balance under the influence of the Planetary Being we know as Uranus. These days and nights of the black and white ray have special energies for other different purposes than numerology, but for anyone born on those days the numbers will still read accurately.

For those who accept the fact of re-incarnation, the Ray energy in influence at the time of death determines the Ray of re-incarnation for that Being's Consciousness, and if a Being dies on the same Ray as the birth Ray, it is an indication that an important item of Karmic obligation has been completed. Once again this is taken into account by the Soul to calculate the next incarnation time and place.

As already stated, there is a chart for the leap year and the non leap year. All discrepancies are ironed out on the 23rd of December, and in the case of a leap year the 22nd of December as well.

I stress the fact that all Avatara (messengers of God to carry the Christ Force) MUST be born on the Black and White ray, and therefore can only be born on the 22nd or 23rd of December. I do realize that this goes against church teaching of most denominations, but that doesn't and cannot ever alter the facts about the Black and White ray.

The following chart is for a NON leap year only.

Division	Day Color	Night Color	Dates
1	Red	Violet	Dec 24-Jan 5
2	Orange	Indigo	Jan 6-Jan 18
3	Yellow	Blue	Jan 19-Jan 31
4	Green	Green	Feb 1-Feb 13
5	Blue	Yellow	Feb 14-Feb 27
6	Indigo	Orange	Feb 28-Mar 12
7	Violet	Red	Mar 13-Mar 26
8	Red	Violet	Mar 27-Apr 8
9	Orange	Indigo	Apr 9-Apr 21
10	Yellow	Blue	Apr 22-May 3
11	Green	Green	May 4-May 16
12	Blue	Yellow	May 17-May 29

13	Indigo	Orange	May 30-Jun 11
14	Violet	Red	Jun 12-Jun 24
15	Red	Violet	Jun 25-Jul 7
16	Orange	Indigo	Jul 8-Jul 20
17	Yellow	Blue	Jul 21-Aug 2
18	Green	Green	Aug 3-Aug 15
19	Blue	Yellow	Aug 16-Aug 28
20	Indigo	Orange	Aug 29-Sept 10
21	Violet	Red	Sept 11-Sept 22
22	Red	Violet	Sept 23-Oct 5
23	Orange	Indigo	Oct 6-Oct 18
24	Yellow	Blue	Oct 19-Oct 31
25	Green	Green	Nov 1-Nov 13
26	Blue	Yellow	Nov 14-Nov 18
27	Indigo	Orange	Nov 19-Dec 9
28	Violet	Red	Dec 10-Dec 22
0	White	Black	Dec 23

As we know, leap year has another day in it, so therefore the chart will then appear as this.

Leap Year Chart

Division	Day Color	Night Color	Dates
1	Red	Violet	Dec 24-Jan 5
2	Orange	Indigo	Jan 6-Jan 18
3	Yellow	Blue	Jan 19-Jan 31

4	Green	Green	Feb 1-Feb 13
5	Blue	Yellow	Feb 14-Feb 27
6	Indigo	Orange	Feb 28-Mar 11
7	Violet	Red	Mar 12-Mar 25
8	Red	Violet	Mar 26-Apr 7
9	Orange	Indigo	Apr 8-Apr 20
10	Yellow	Blue	Apr 21-May 2
11	Green	Green	May 3-May 15
12	Blue	Yellow	May 16-May 28
13	Indigo	Orange	May 29-Jun 10
14	Violet	Red	Jun 11-Jun 23
15	Red	Violet	Jun 24-Jul 6
16	Orange	Indigo	Jul 7-Jul 19
17	Yellow	Blue	Jul 20-Aug 1
18	Green	Green	Aug 2-Aug 14
19	Blue	Yellow	Aug 15-Aug 27
20	Indigo	Orange	Aug 28-Sept 9
21	Violet	Red	Sept 10-Sept 21
22	Red	Violet	Sept 22-Oct 4
23	Orange	Indigo	Oct 5-Oct 17
24	Yellow	Blue	Oct 18-Oct 30
25	Green	Green	Oct 31-Nov 12
26	Blue	Yellow	Nov 13-Nov 27
27	Indigo	Orange	Nov 28-Dec 8
28	Violet	Red	Dec 9-Dec 21
0	White	Black	Dec 22-Dec 23

ACCURACY OF NUMEROLOGY

Illustrating a point about accuracy, some years ago I had the occasion to do the numerology of the son of a doctor. This doctor worked for a 900-bed hospital where I was in attendance performing my daily duties. After my giving the reading, this doctor said I was completely wrong and way out of sync with her son's personality. Thinking I may have made an error, I double-checked on my reading and it was correct. Rather cheekily I stated that this person obviously did not know her son very well, which as you can imagine rather got up her nose somewhat and called me a rather uncomplimentary name. For three days this went on with this doctor niggling me and telling me I was wrong, and for these days I insisted the numbers were right. After this time the doctor said that she was just seeing if I was really convinced of my subject, and that she was checking to see if the reading may have been a fluke, because everything I had said was spot-on in accuracy regarding her son's personality. We became very good friends after that little episode.

Before starting on the numbers themselves, I am going to drive you mad through this book with reminding you at various places that there is not such a thing as a fully positive or negative person. We all have our positive and negative moments, but we normally revert to one or the other when under pressure, and this is where we show up our numerology pattern in a very certain way. This is a very important point to remember.

We shall begin to start on the numbers and work through them one at a time. **I would suggest that you read one number at a time and work on it for a couple**

of days before progressing to the next number. Over the years of teaching this art, I have found that this seems to be the easiest and best way of getting the meanings into the mind of pupils, and locked down solid.

3	6	9
2	5	8
1	4	7

I usually use a simple zeros and crosses pattern for the chart, but because I am printing this with the computer it is easier to make a grid box pattern. Look at the zeros and crosses style or grid pattern above. You will see that all the numbers have their own square. The numbers must always be put in their designated position. They are never added together, but put in their original single units. You will notice that zeros are also used and not discarded as it is advocated by so many other numerology systems. To demonstrate this point of placement of numbers, let us imagine that we are going to read the birth date of 11-2-1978 (February 11). Then in this case the three ones shall be in the same bottom left-hand square shown below.

		9
2		8
111		7

The birth date shall be divided into the day numbers 11, the month number 2, the year number 78, and the century number 19, giving the 11-2-1978 birth date. Right from the outset we must understand that the day figures are the strongest figures, followed by the month figures, year figures and century figures respectively. This important point will never vary. The name figures will be even weaker than the century figures, but nevertheless they will have certain energies to put into the personality.

⚠ I am now going to explain my use of the term Schizophrenic that I use throughout this book. The true meaning of this word does NOT mean mad, but just a division of personality. Leave us not confuse the true meaning of this word, by using it in the now popularly used (or more often abused) way for depicting a so-called madness or mental problem.

Now if the birth date lacks 3.5.7., or lacks 4.5.6. or 1.5.9. the person will be what is called Schizophrenic. Remember this is NOT madness or mental but simply a division of personality, however if this exists with other problems, then it will certainly cause mental stress. As you can see from the Grid above, the lack of the three numbers 4.5.6 will make a vacant gap. This gap makes it hard for the coupling of the forces to work together as one. The same applies for 3.5.7 and 1.5.9. You can now see from the chart above that the birth date 11-2-1978 lacks 4.5.6. indicating the trend towards a schizophrenic personality. This is an indication that a 5 name would be most desirable to soften the tendency of Schizophrenia. A 5 name will not eliminate this tendency, but it can surely make the schizophrenic effect of frustration far weaker if the name is changed to give the 5 at a young enough age. The reason why a name change can alter the psyche is that we visualize our name in our mind every time we are called it. Although this is done unconsciously, it still has an effect on our mental being. Trying a name change on a 50 year old person however will not produce much effect due to the habitual registering of the name over the past 50 years.

Energies can flow in vertical, horizontal or the diagonal lines of 3.5.7 and 1.5.9 throughout the grid, but they will not flow from 2-6, 6-8, 8-4, 4-2 or vice versa. It will therefore be noticed that energy from the 5 will flow to all numbers equally and therefore readily couple each and every number together.

Remember that we stated the energies can only flow vertical, horizontal, or across 3.5.7 line or 1.5.9. line. It is because of this the 5 would bind all the numbers together if there was one present, which there is not. This gap is an inhibiting factor in the transmission of energies between the numbers. Gaps are most important and must always be read and not ignored as is done by many systems.

The Name is important to the life of the personality. It helps or hinders the smooth working of the character. Using the name alone as some numerologists suggest cannot assess the basic character. The name can be changed where the birth date cannot. As stated before, a name change can assist the personality to control certain aspects of its being, but it cannot change the basics of the personality.

The name of a person has its best effect if used right from birth throughout life. This matters not if it is their correct name or a nickname, the effect will be the same as long as it is the normal name that is constantly in use.

With wisdom and knowledge the parents can make up for shortcomings in their child's personality by wise choice of name or nickname; for instance any child born without any of the Schizophrenic gap numbers can remedy this by choosing a name that vibrates to 5. This instantly (albeit very weakly) assists the child in overcoming any deficiency of personality. Naturally a 5 is not always desirable, and in some instances would be quite undesirable, but it may be that there is another number that would benefit the personality to a great extent.

Of course the Entity will already have prior knowledge of whether the future parents could or would do this anyhow and would be taken into account. To calculate the name number, add the numbers of the letters in the name.

No matter what language or alphabet, the numbers are always continued to the last letter in rotation of nine. This works because 9 is the perfect number; we will discuss this fact later.

The vowels = the Soul's ideals and expression.

The consonants = the impressions made in the seen world.

The total = the true vibrational rate of the name.

```
A B C D E F G H I    J K L M N O P Q R    S T U V W X Y Z
1 2 3 4 5 6 7 8 9    1 2 3 4 5 6 7 8 9    1 2 3 4 5 6 7 8
```

therefore

```
JOHN          JON          JONN          JONNE
1 6 8 5=20=2  1 6 5=12=3   1 6 5 5=17=8  1 6 5 5 5=22=4
```

This indicates how the name number is derived. The surname is irrelevant as it is the name you are most called that vibrates to your personality. If you had the nickname of Butch and every one called you that, then you would use that name to calculate the vibrational number.

BUTCH
2 3 2 3 8=18=9 As you can see, if the normal name was John or any other of the spellings shown, then the name Butch would have a totally different vibration altogether.

Wise parents will think on this before they name their newborn children, and give them the best advantage for the coming lifetime. When numerology indicates that a change of name is a distinct advantage, it should be regarded as important to adjust the vibration to a new name, or at least a different spelling of your present name to alter the vibration to a more beneficial one to suit your own needs. The vibratory effect comes from the person mentally visualizing their name, even though they do not realize they always do this when they are called by that name.

3	6	9
2	5	8
1	4	7

Note in the grid above these numbers 3.6.9 represent mental or spiritual side, 2.5.8. represent the emotional side, and the 1.4.7. represent the physical side of our personalities.

Numbers used together like 4.5.6 are on the line of Earth, 1.5.9. Air, 3.5.7 Fire, and 2.5.8. Water.

The numbers 2.5.8 lacking in the birth date will indicate that the personality is never willing to tell or show their deepest emotional feeling to any person unless they are very close, and even then it is rare that they disclose this fully. Lack of these numbers indicate that such a person feels comfortable when floating in water, like swimming or taking baths often. This is the trait of the emotions, which operate on the Astral or Spiritual level.

With the numbers 4.5.6. lacking, this creates frustration on the earth line. As a result of this I have found that all people I have read with this gap do derive a deep sense of inner comfort when they are actively engaged in working in the garden, or walking barefoot in contact with the soil. The soil seems to have some close affinity with these people and the planetary vibration seems to soothe them in some way.

Now it is possible that the situation arises where the numbers flow in a circle such as 12-3-1964. They will be placed in the grid thus:

3	6	9
2		8
11	4	

Let us imagine the hypothetical birth-date 12-3-1964. When the numbers are put into the grid properly, it can be seen that coupling of the energy via the numbers can only be done in a virtual circle. It is obviously taking the long way round the grid's edge in a circular fashion. This will indicate quite clearly that the personality will always do things the long way around without taking shortcuts. The same will occur if the birth-date also is 13-2-1946 as they show exactly the same numbers in the grid, but the strength of the numbers is in different places with each date. Both personalities will still do things the long way around.

Before we delve into the individual numbers, here is a chart of basic meanings. Don't worry about this too much at this point as we will deal with all the numbers separately to ensure proper understanding.

Pure numerology uses the standard numerals of society to assess the traits the spirit has chosen to use in this incarnation.

0. God unmanifest: Whole and undivided, life not yet started for mankind.
1. God wills: Life, as mankind knows it, starts = determination.
2. God Loves: = Adaptability.
3. God gives life: Desire for personal self-expression.
4. Love manifests: Human goes into action.
5. Mankind needs balance: Calculating critical mind.
6. Balance needs choice: Free will in action, seeker seeks truth.
7. Choice needs sacrifice: Ability to give, strength in decision.
8. Sacrifice needs Love: Mankind learning love knows no hurt.
9. Love needs wisdom: Knowing = spirituality in action and application.
0. Wisdom finds God: we return to God through experience of limitation.

Positive aspects:
1. Initiative, positive, determined, persistent, good mental and physical health, strong balanced thinking, originator.

2. Cooperative, charming, helpful, optimistic, energetic, visually creative, clairvoyant, peacemaker, diplomat.
3. Religious, spiritual, artistic, accurate, eye for detail, clever, brainy, desires self-expression, power of generation.
4. Manifests thoughts and ideas, builder, stamina and good health, adept with hands and body, gains through opportunity, politician.
5. Controlled energy, balanced thinking and action, calculating thinker, clairaudience, salesman, adventurer.
6. Thinker, planner, thinks with reason to find facts and knowledge, experimenter with life, teacher, parent, doctor.
7. Positive, capable, self-reliant, accepts self, sensitive, sacrifice with love—especially for family, perfectionist.
8. Dominant, strong, forceful, driving personality, loves deeply and passionately, sensitive and tactful, feeling psychic, promoter.
9. Deep inner wisdom, patient, gentle, kind, intuitive, loves people and truth, philanthropist, traveller, healer, minister.
0. The ability to succeed when the heart and mind are in one accord, strong, determined to have successful achievement.

Negative aspects:
1. Inferiority complex (if only one 1), four or more ones: stubborn, rigid thinking and bad health.
2. Emotional, easily led, changeable, too adaptable, doormat, nervy, unstable, unreliable, unreliable psychic, careless.

3. Narrow-minded, selfish and demanding, pessimism, finicky and fussy, bogged down in detail, bigoted, false pride, extravagance.
4. Slovenly, wasteful of opportunities, sensual, heavy physical expression, rigidity, sternness, restriction, false pride.
5. Wastes energy, restless, calculatingly mercenary, given to criticism, changeability, irresponsibility, mixed up psychic.
6. Slow thinker, introspective, worrier, anxiety, problem maker, moody, sullen, fearful, argumentative, mental illness.
7. Possessive, jealous, selfish, defensively cruel, sarcasm, coldness, humiliation, fearful of being hurt, melancholy.
8. Emotionally domineering, tastelessly cruel to sadistic, self-destructive, turns off love, cannot face others, aggressive, impatient, intolerant, ruthless, scheming, fearful psychic.
9. Cannot cope with the flow of intuitive knowledge, mental emotional frustration, withdrawn, lacks mental strength, selfishness, indiscreet, bitterness, vice.
0. Obstinate, dominates, refuse to see truth, personal desires uppermost, fanaticism, dishonesty.

As we progress through the numbers, I suggest you get pencil and paper ready, and draw the examples into the chart if there is no example already within these notes, and you can then readily see the effects of gaps and coupling. This practice will stand you in good stead.

NUMBER ONE

It is now time to attack the subject of the numbers themselves. We shall start with the number one in the positive and negative sides of that number. If any birth date has several of the same numbers within the birth date, that trait will be strengthened in the personality. This can be over-done to a point of detriment and is not always a good thing. We will see this as we progress along the numbers.

POSITIVE ONE

The positive one has determination and necessary ability and initiative to satisfactorily carry out any project started. They are definite in their ideas of what is right and wrong and at the same time very purposeful in their ways. They strongly follow and believe in social and moral laws of life. If they have strong ones, i.e. three or more, they have a great tendency to live in a black or white situation, with no bending either way. Factual and down to earth in all their assessments, they are found to be dependable in all

24

they say or do. Their word is their bond and they stick to the decision made, even if the result is against them. Such a level of positivity does not allow for much adaptability. They are the strong silent types who show their thinking through their deeds rather than their speech. They love deeply, strongly and reliably, for they are not fickle. Being very undemonstrative, they are often accused of being hard, unloving, or lacking in love, and only thinking of what they want out of life. This is not true, and they should be assessed through their ability to help others.

Balanced positive ones, i.e. 2 to 4 ones depending upon their position in the birth date, are good clear thinkers and actors. They have the ability to come up with new ideas and put them into practice, especially if aided by a 2, 3, or 5 and particularly if they have all three. The 2 and 5 give a pliability to an otherwise rigid and unbendable nature. The 3 adds extra mental ability with loyalty thrown in, but we will deal with these other figures later.

When positive even to the point of having too many ones, the one character is thoughtful and compassionate, feeling deeply the problems of others. They always advocate the necessary practical steps needed to overcome the difficulties which surround others. They are good leaders in business for they have the common sense and the ability to control and direct what needs to be done to succeed. They have a keen sense of buying and selling, and their natural initiative and persistence gives them dominion over the circumstances they control. They are definite and progressive people.

NEGATIVE ONE

The negative one has two extremes, namely "the century one" which shows an inferiority complex, which is an inability to maintain personal self-confidence in self-judgment, or their natural abilities. Too often they give others the pleasure of making their decisions for them, even in the small things of life, and they reflect the desire of others in what they do. Failure comes in indecisiveness, hesitancy, lack of initiative, confidence in self and/or persistence just when they could succeed. They tend to give up just when success is near at hand. Fear is their problem and this causes them to be shy, or an aggressive front to disguise this shyness, which they view as weakness. Fear of failure, ridicule or possible mistakes often stops them before they start.

Love is a problem, for they desire to be loved rather than love actively giving of themselves. They succumb easily to rebuffs. If coupled with an eight they will fluctuate from shyness and self-effacing attitudes to that of aggressiveness and drive to compensate for the inferiority. This aggressiveness is often mistaken for determination.

Determination is of the mind, not the emotions. Clear thinking allows appropriate action, while emotional reaction is defensiveness and leads to obstinacy, a negative reaction.

In the other extreme, we have too many ones, and this brings about a narrowing of the outlook, and a slow thinking attitude causing, at best, a hardening or limiting of the thinking abilities, tending to slow pedantic mental activity, demanding black and white decisions in every situation. Lacking pliability, they are adamant, obstinate, pigheaded, narrow-minded, and refuse to adjust. They lack leadership as they lack pliability and fail because of rigidity of thinking and purpose.

Love is a problem and though strong in their love, they expect others to know they love them, not needing to be told constantly. They show their depth of love in the practical things they do for the family and others. Change comes about by planting a thought in their mind and letting them think about it for a week or more, then they come up with the idea which was put to them a week or so before. They need time to think before they put things into action.

The layout of the chart is in the normal zeros and crosses design, and each number must always be put into its right space.

3 6 9 The top line represents the mental and spiritual aspects.

2 5 8 The middle line represents the emotional and E.S.P. factors.

1 4 7 The bottom line represents the physical factors.

The individual birth date figures must always be placed in the correct space; therefore a date of 11-11-1911 means that there are seven ones in this birth date and all these ones must be put in the appropriate space.

		9
111111		

The 9 shows mental and spiritual dexterity and sensitivity.

The lack of 4.5.6. and also 3.5.7. shows the Schizophrenic tendency.

The lack of emotional figures 2.5.8. shows lack of emotional expression.

The seven ones show extreme pedantic obstinacy, narrow-mindedness, and rigid thinking.

It is here I would like to discuss a point of positivity. Having ones is like adding a stronger will to a personality. There comes a point where, if too many are added, the will becomes so strong that it is so taken up with being forceful that it becomes narrow and bigoted. Imagine a small torch globe that is attached to a battery without the torch reflector. Such a meagre glow would not light up any large building. Now if we put this into a torch where the beam could be focused, we would see a beam cutting through the distance and clearly light up what it was aimed at. All outside that beam would still be in darkness. This is like the ones: the more ones, the more focused the beam is, BUT the more narrow and inflexible is the beam of thinking. This gives a narrow beam of narrow-mindedness in one direction without being able to change in any way. This is the indication of a narrow-minded bigot. In the date above we would now see that the personality is narrow-minded, stubborn, pigheaded, with schizophrenic tendencies and would not be able to show emotion. Such a person would tend to think they are the center of the world, and indeed this would be so for them. Such a person would be almost impossible to live with, and sadly I found a situation where this birth date applied to one man (11-11-1921) who made his wife's life a pure hell. This however is an extreme case.

The individual power of each figure is the position in the birth date. The day figure is the strongest aspect of the personality; the month figures are not as strong as the day figures. The year figures are not as strong as the month figures, and the century figures are the weakest of all. If we look at the example we are using, i.e. 11-11-1911, we can see how these figures represent the basic power and activity of the individual who has chosen this birth date as the tools with which it will use as its character in this incarnation.

The century figure one, being very weak, shows an inferiority complex. Add a year one to the century one, and we have added strength to the one aspect, but because the year figure is not a strong figure in itself, we still have a certain amount of inferiority mixed with the determination. If we add another year figure, so that now we have three ones, we have reasonable determination and persistence. These three ones are equal to the strength of a century one and a month one.

A century one plus a month one shows nice determination and persistence, but able to change the mind if the reason is sufficiently good enough. The century one plus a day one shows good determination and persistence and is stronger than a month combination.

A century one with two month ones shows very good determination and persistence, but with the possibility to change the mind and direction if necessary.

A century one plus two day ones show very good determination and persistence, but with enough rigidity to have difficulty in changing the mind. If a person has a century one and a total of three ones, then they have reasonably good determination; if four ones, then they have a tendency to obstinacy, and if five ones or more, then a nature given to rigidity of thought and action and because of this limitation has a negative aspect due to narrow thinking channels.

In this particular character, there are no emotional figures, and this shows great frustration and limitation of communicating with others, consequently this limitation with the over abundance of ones, makes the personality even more stiff and rigid, making for a life of frustration in character and work place.

No 4.5.6. is a limiting of emotional and mental expression but not as limiting as the lack of 2.5.8. No 3.5.7. is a milder restriction, but limits the personality's expression to communicate with others. Each of these rifts can be overcome partly by name vibrations which will be dealt with later. The division is called schiz-o-phrenia which literally means divided in self, but is NOT MENTALLY ILL as some medical "experts" would say. Each of these divisions can cause a natural frustration, and the results can be very changeable personalities of varying degrees, according to positivity or knowledge on the subject. Numerology can help overcome some of these problems.

	6	9
111	4	7

If we have a personality with good strong ones, e.g. 11- 4-1967, the problem of division is apparent, but this personality is not a negative character, for they are normally very positive and have the ability to adjust to some degree to the inability to express themselves emotionally. They would of course have difficulty in communicating socially, but would be able to do so with an employer where the conversation is about work and does not involve the emotions. Only when the emotions are not being used can this personality express without fear of the emotional reaction that comes with this problem. This person is physically oriented because of the ones and the great determination and persistence; the four shows physical dexterity and adeptness with the hands and body. The seven gives them the added ability to go after the things they personally want in life, also a desire for the family life.

Remember no person is ever always positive or negative, but will vary according to the pressure they are under. The more pressure they receive, the more they revert to their basic numerology. Anyone can be positive without any pressure, but pressure or stress brings out the basic

NUMBER TWO

We shall now endeavour to examine the attributes of the two. This is a very important number from the flexibility, adaptability, and psychic side of things.

As with all numbers, we have a positive and negative side.

POSITIVE TWO

To be a positive two, the two must have at least two positive ones, i.e. the ones must come from the month or day figures, seldom from the year figures unless born on the 11 day and 11 month, which would be needed to gain the positivity required to manage the twos of the year. Born on the second day of the month, the positive two shows the inherent creative ability to take the blueprint of the ideas and thoughts of others and give them clothing raiment of the visible physical world. The two can transmute spirit into matter.

If the two has a four to assist it, the personality will be practical and very capable in any field, developing the natural skills of the craftsman and the highly developed tradesman.

Women also do the same in their chosen field of endeavour, for they would be the doer not the architect. If a six is with the two, then the two becomes an architect not a doer, an inventor not a labourer. They have very progressive ideas, and with guidance can make the most of their assets. This is by giving of themselves for the good of others and the community. They love freely and easily and are generous with their time, energy and thoughts.

Because of the adaptability of the two, they seldom want to be top dog, rather playing second fiddle and feeding the ego of their employer or marriage partner.

Being optimistic they tend to be of a forgiving nature, but they turn off their love just as easily as it is turned on, for they seldom love deeply, and they react emotionally to adverse thoughts and actions of others. When others love them, they love strongly and passionately, even possessively, but when the passion dies they wish to be free. They want to love without being tied too strongly by personal attachments and it takes the added strength of other specialized combinations of figures to offset these reactions.

They are sympathetic and seldom selfish, for they feel the need to express the feelings of mind and the emotions, both orally and physically. They find it a bore if they have demanded of them more than they want to give willingly.

The two is naturally clairvoyant, but in most people this is usually well suppressed by unbelieving parents, society and/or the environment. If properly trained, they can be inspired, accurate within their capabilities, and very helpful in time of need for others. They think with their heart, not with the mind.

NEGATIVE TWO

A negative two compounds a negative one into a state of abject apathy regarding their own abilities. They have an excessive doormat problem, for they tend to let other people ride rough-shod over them. This is even to the degree that they live life only in the shadow of another's personality, reflecting only the decisions of others. They seldom make a true lasting effort to change the situation, preferring to remain meek and mild with an inferiority complex. They seldom even protest, but when they do, it is usually with a display of really bad temper, which upsets everyone and in so doing often destroys valuable friendships. When they calm down, they return to the doormat position and expect others to forget and forgive.

Usually very psychic but unreliable, for they do not separate their negativity from what they see and hear. If control assisted by a positive personality, they could become good authors, actors, doctors, nurses etc., as the positive two is. They could also develop a diagnostic x-ray vision. Such a diagnostic x-ray vision is not only able to see the aura, but can actually see within the person's physical body just like a normal x-ray machine. This is a very unique ability developed by no other number that I know of, and because of the rarity of those who can develop this talent to its full potential, will seldom be believed possible by those who cannot do it themselves.

They are also referred to as highly strung people, but this is not so. They just do not control their emotional nerves. They become emotionally sick with pseudo coughs, colds, flu, asthma, bronchitis, heart problems, stomach aches, pains etc. Worry creates the problem. Men tend to the above, while women blame God for pains in childbirth and menstrual period problems. Both suffer from nerves and ulcers. Both can be subject to almost uncontrollable fears of almost anything; their imagination is too good for their own good. The not so negative are easily influenced by others, whether good or bad personalities, and are easily led to think and act as others want them to. Reason and intuition often war in the negative two, and frustration causes them to lack the initiative to make decisions, or give strength to a contrary argument. Negative two's merely reflect the surroundings they are in, instantly and perfectly. Their love is of the fawning and doting kind, shallow and lacking strength.

The layout of the chart is in the usual manner of the zeros and crosses, remembering that the power of the figures remains the same in all cases, i.e. the day figure is strongest, then the month figure, then the year, and finally the century. The difference from here on is that, unlike the ones which grow in strength and power to control the personality by an addition of ones, any addition of the twos results in a negative aspect, which can usually only be offset by the strength supplied by additional ones to the character. (This aspect also applies to all other figures.)

The following first example shows the ability of the ones to give strength to the two and to supply all the positive qualities the two is capable of. The second example, however, does not give the same strength to the two as the first one does, due to the century one being so weak.

2-11-1987

		9
2		8
111		7

12-8-1964

	6	9
2		8
11	4	

2-11-1987 or 12-8-1964—both of these two charts of figures would be enhanced by having a name, which adds to five. This is quite obvious from the schizophrenic gaps in both grids, which does not allow the flow of energies through all the numbers. The moral code would come to 2 in the first grid and 3 in the second grid. The first grid would gain no useful effect in cancelling the schizophrenic gap to allow the energy to flow freely. In the second grid, however, the moral code would assist in flow of energy, but it would be the long way around, but nonetheless would slightly assist the flow easing the frustration tendencies of the personality.

		9
22		8
111		

This set of figures in the chart above, 22-8-1911, despite the number of ones in it, would be offset by the power of the two's, and the lack of 4.5.6., making a gap in the chart, would certainly not help any. The two's are too strong for the weak year and century ones. The personality would have a constant struggle to maintain a steady balanced effect, for the emotional tendency is to think with the heart, and not the mind, yet the personality would not be described as a negative personality, but would certainly have to watch the tendency to drop into the state of negative thinking. A day two is a strong and powerful figure and would assist a positive personality to be adaptable, and in control of the adaptability. It gives strong influence to sharpen the ability of thinking; it adds speed to the perception through the mind and the intuition. This is a visual creative perception, which, if accompanied with a four, makes the personality also physically capable of putting their ideas into a see-able form. This would apply to month two also, but to a lesser degree. Year two's would mostly be subject to the influence of the other figures in the personality chart.

Two two's as in 22-1-1911 are the ruling factors in this personality, but would be offset to some degree by the build up of the power of the ones to control, but again we find the difficulty is that the perception of the two twos constantly tries to overcome the commonsense of the ones. Also lacking a five, the personality would be plagued by the constant problem of division, and this would create frustration, with indecision being a major factor in the emotional thinking. A five name would play a very important role in giving a positive attitude that would allow this personality to give their creative best.

If we transpose the above figures to be this, 12-2-1911, the personality would be more stable than if born on the 22nd and the background moral lessons would also be of positive value to the personality. Again a five name would be an essential ingredient to the smooth working of the personality.

22-2-1922

		9
22222		
1		

22-2-1922 is a negatively reacting personality, for the simple fact that the personality will be ruled by the emotional reaction to life and the situations it would be involved in. If given a responsible position in industry, would have to be watched very carefully to see that they did not change things which are proven assets and working properly, to something they dream up in their imagination. They need to be given the right to discuss their ideas with other responsible people, who can assess the merits of their inventive thinking. Note the Gap of 3.5.7. and 4.5.6., making things once again very difficult.

Usually the tendency of these personalities is to grow up already accepting they are no good at anything, and that they just live life simply because they are in it. They would, as a general rule, accept life as it is and go along with what is happening, for they would be optimistic most of the time. If pessimistic, they would be petulant and abusive about almost anything which spells of law and order, simply because it would be too restrictive for them. They would be changeable and unreliable, and not separate their negative personality from their perceptions of what they do. Many of these people would live in a constant state of day-dreaming and think this is normal. Psychiatrists will make a fortune from these unfortunate people who cannot turn off their natural clairvoyance.

2-6-1936

3	66	9
2		
1		

Reading this number 2-6-1936 we would see straight off that there is an inferiority complex due to only having a very weak century one. The grid also shows that this personality will do everything the long way around as shown by all the numbers running around the outside edge of the grid. This personality would be a natural worrier and particularly in small things. The six makes them morbid and morose about the things they are involved in, and would, if not taught properly at an early age, delve into psychic phenomena and most likely experiment with black magic, then, because of the three and the pair of sixes and the nine, need psychiatric care believing they are possessed of evil spirits. As a lot of orthodox medicine and religion are only too ready to believe this as I have before stated, and because of this popular but erroneous belief, it is very hard to help these people help themselves. Of course we do occasionally strike the enlightened members of religion and medicine at times, but unfortunately this is indeed a rarity.

The 22-3-1933, 22-6-1966, 22-9-1966, 22-3-1966, 2-12-1936 and 2-6-1999 are all simple examples of the way a two personality can and will be ruled by the mental figures of the personality. It is almost infallible to say that each of the above personalities would have to have psychiatric care at least once in their lifetime.

NUMBER THREE

POSITIVE THREE

The basis of three, whether positive or negative, is the desire for individual personal expression. The three is the life that gives life to life, the Power of The Holy Spirit in action. It is the instinctive mother action, which gives of its own life that new life be sustained.

A three has a brilliant mind, a clever mind, geared to use the full knowledge reliably and accurately in constructive detail just like a computer. It thrives on the beauty of accuracy in all things. It does not like mistakes. The three needs a two to enable it to freely express, by giving speed and visional capacity to the thoughts. The three coupled with a five gives a critical and calculating honesty, while coupled to a six gives the ability to think and plan with reason.

Threes are capable of succeeding in a wide range of projects and activities. They do best when concentrating on a single project with the full capacity and accuracy of their mind. They are one-pointed both in thinking and acting.

When born on the third, they are usually happiest working in the company of others. They certainly like to be the center of attention. They excel as salesmen/women, politicians playing with the destinies of people, or in the ministry, anywhere they can laud it over others. These people are artists in the true sense of the word, for they can make everything they touch beautiful and they like their talents to be seen and recognized. They will very readily admit how good they are to all who enquire, and also to those who don't enquire.

A good business mind, accountancy suits them, as do other jobs which employ accuracy of mind and action. Science, pharmacy, law and government posts attract them. Law and order is their forte, and are good teachers if not bogged down in detail. They are extremely loyal to themselves and their personal ideas, also to those they love and cherish, and to those they work with. They are religious and high-minded and often psychic without any other psychic figures.

NEGATIVE THREE

These personalities are finicky and fussy, unable to see the wood for the trees. They get lost in detail and consequently see only the details they wish to, without seeing the major parts. They see the surface not the substance. Bogged down in detail they become narrow and bigoted in most things when mind and heart are controlling the actions.

If ailing, they keep the sickness alive by the constant reliving of every detail to an incredible degree. They do not realize that they help manifest and keep alive the woes that beset them, for they do not believe they have the power to control any part of their life and mostly refuse to even try. Quite often fear of the unknown causes inaction. If only one 1, and there are three or more 3s, they will fluctuate from extreme accuracy in employment to downright slovenliness at work and at home, yet will demand the accuracy and the tidiness they are capable of from others. This weak character aspect works in reverse and is demanding and perverse and bigoted in thought and action especially if accompanied by a seven, for then they are also possessive and jealous. With sixes they are too introspective and worry over trifles. With nines they cannot cope with the down-pouring of divine ideas. When two or more threes are coupled with sixes or nines, it is a foregone conclusion that they will have bouts of mental illness. If psychic they have to be watched for exaggeration and untruths.

The negative desires to be noticed and will use minute details to hold the attention or to show that they are either so brainy that they can see more than others, or to show that they have no control over the situation. They put on airs and graces to impress, yet are true cynics and carry stupid loyalty to embarrassing extremes. Personal self-control of the mind and all its activities is a must for these personalities. When you have two or more threes, and any sort of division in the personality such as no 3.5.7 (fire line), or 4.5.6 (earth line), or 1.5.9 (air line), then it is almost certain that this personality will take every chance to seek praise for everything they do. They will even change the conversation to a point where it is almost impossible not to comment on how good or very clever they have been. They soak this up and demand more while continually denying they wish to have any limelight. If there's the gap, and they also have two eights, they will also get very cranky if they are not given what they regard is their just respect and praise, and they will get quite nasty accusing people of trying to take all their limelight away. They will go to incredible lengths to get their praise, and actually make fools of themselves in so doing. Of course they cannot see this for themselves, but to others around them it is very demanding and tiring.

Two threes will be loyal to an embarrassing extreme to anyone they choose to put as worthy of their merit, and they will remain loyal unless confronted by absolute proof that the other person is unworthy of such loyalty.

As is usual, the day figure is always the strongest and has more influence as a single unit than any other unit in the birth-date. A very strong three can also be the thirteenth or the thirty-first, while the month figure can only be a three. Year figures are weak. The year figure can of course be 3, 30, 13, or 31 etc., but these figures do not have the power to influence the month or day figures much, even when they are doubled. Nevertheless each figure adds to the strength of the others in the same denomination, so that a strong day three can be turned negative by the addition of two year threes. This is because the three then becomes overdone, and if not offset by strong ones, will naturally be negative in action.

Born on the 3-3-1933 certainly shows the narrowing effect of the three and bigotry will result from these figures. The 6-3-1933 like the first set of threes will develop mental stress that can cause need for psychiatric care at some stage, but the six will have an alleviating effect on the narrowness of the threes. These personalities need name figures which will offset the abundance of the threes. Physical name vibrations probably do more to offset the problem, but we must make sure that the personality has an emotional figure to join the mind to the physical, or the addition of a physical figure to balance the threes will have little effect.

Emotional figures often accentuate any heavy mental stress due to an over abundance of threes rather than offset the problem. An example is 8-5-1933 or 8-3-1933—these emotions would accentuate, but the accentuation would be more acute with 3-3-1958, 85, 28, 82 as year figures.

The three to be a positive three, and have all the attributes of this positive number, needs to be a single three, with at least two ones, or a maximum of two three's and a minimum of three ones, and in all cases there must be joining figures to allow for freedom of expression, e.g. 13-5-1927, 15-3-1927, 13-5-1926 or 3-12-1936. If these figures are put into the chart in the usual way, you will see the power of the ones to control and stabilize. You will also see the freedom of expression offsets any tendency to negativity, allowing the positive forces to act fully depending on environment and personal pressures in the work and family situations.

It must always be remembered that although parents do not give the personality its characteristic traits, they do have strong influence over the developing personality and that influence is as positive or negative as their own personal training or learning. All children are taught by the personal views around them—parents, all relatives, teachers and society as a whole, and their own particular in-built traits. Personal observation allows us to see that some very positive personalities are weakened by very negative environment, while the opposite is also quite possible, however the original effect of the date of birth tries to shine through. In situations of this kind only experience in the art of numerology can get the true personality, and like all skills there is no substitute for experience.

The positive three is usually a trustworthy individual whose loyalty is to be relied upon. They have a quick brain, which is clever, artistic and accurate in all they do. While they demand personal self-expression, they like to do that which is right in preference to demanding their own right.

As with all figures the combinations are almost endless, and it is only practice, which makes for perfection of reading numerology. This is where the three excels, for they delight in their accuracy for detail, and all their effort is put into achieving as much perfection as time and effort and circumstance will allow. Both the positive and negative three apply themselves in this way. It is only a case of direction, for each will succeed in the direction chosen.

It is well that we never forget that each of us have chosen the personality we have, and it is the means by which we apply ourselves to life, and by which we assess the circumstances and events around us. The three personality's action and reaction high-light the fact that we do have pre-destiny insofar as we (our true spirit) seeks its goal in life, and we still have free will in the framework of that destiny to choose and direct the means of our seeking, even while we consciously or unconsciously travel the path to our goal. This applies to all personalities regardless of whether they have weak or strong personality, for no other person can live the life for another. We can help, encourage and even push hard occasionally, but in the end it is the personality concerned that must do the making of its own decisions. This is one of the unchanging principles of life and it must be so, no matter whether we like it or not.

NUMBER FOUR

POSITIVE FOUR

Born on the 4th, 14th, or the 24th day of the month, these personalities are usually trustworthy and reliable. With the day figure being the strongest influence in the personality, they have a very practical approach to life and its needs.

The motto for other people to follow is to turn to this person when in trouble, for they will guide and help in a practical manner. They are usually very good people who are calm and balanced in their approach to life and the reality of the things that need to be achieved. They are down-to-earth practical people, who use the physical approach to the problems of life.

The four personality will like the good things of life, and their aim is to get them, yet they value their reputation, so are very prudent and careful as to how they achieve what they want. They are proud of their physical and mental capabilities and are extremely adept with their hands and their body. They like physical action, for it is an outlet that is used to relieve mental and emotional stresses.

Being sensitive to the physical conditions that surrounds them, their spirituality is shown in duty and the desire to live according to the spiritual and social laws. Sound judgment is used in social niceties and where etiquette is concerned.

Usually ambitious in the physical sense, they are tireless workers in their quest to succeed, especially when that bit of personal effort is necessary. They have confidence in themselves and the persistence to succeed. They are try-ers in the real sense of the word, for they give it a go. They make the opportunity they need, or they have the opportunity given to them, and they use it to their best advantage.

True, they often tend to use up their personal resources, both materially and emotionally. They do this through their steadfastness to the objective and with their impatience with the mundane in life, yet they maintain good health, for they have good recuperative power if they make sure they get enough rest. They usually like short fingernails, right back to the quick for two reasons: 1. to have more sensitive fingertips to feel into the work they are doing—like a surgeon, or doing fine production work; 2. to be able to more delicately love the opposite sex.

NEGATIVE FOUR

Negative fours are willful in their attitude and demands that others do for them. They are hard taskmasters, tending to rule by dogged determination and obstinacy, with no allowances for the inabilities of others to live up to what they think is their own standards. If strong willed, they will use their will deliberately, destructively both in thought and action; especially will they rebel against law and order. The rules of life bore them, and they desire to be a law unto themselves. They are blind to the effect of Karma. They do not believe moral lessons that fit them for a higher life. They believe in one life and that the world owes them a living, and rarely believe that life continues beyond the grave.

If weak, they hate the mundane and deliberately look for change for the sake of change. They show their impatience with those they think dull and boring people, especially if coupled with 6s or 5s.

When weak, they lack the concentration to achieve the object of their desires. They are careless, unreliable, and often downright stupid in thought and action, declaring that God made them as they are and they cannot change themselves for other people or society. For them spirituality in the real sense does not exist. Any illness is usually a true physical illness, i.e. an organic problem, and should be treated as such with pills and potions, for these personalities need doctors.

If the illness is emotional, the result will be physical. If the illness is of mental origin, it will still become a physical illness. Though spiritual healing works with them as with all other people, it is not openly acceptable as feasible, therefore it is pooh-poohed and not often sought after.

The 4 needs the help of other figures to become imaginative. One of the major things to be noticed with the positive 4s is the practical spirituality of the personality, especially when they have most of their figures in the physical plane. They are usually more spiritual in the practical sense than those who are oriented in the emotional and mental areas of the chart.

The following examples show the strengths of the 4 in the different positions.

The day 4.   4-11-1953 (moral code 4, karmic lesson 6). The 4 rules the aspect of the ones and directs their determination and persistence to achieve practical results. The mental three gives artistic accuracy, the five down-to-earth balance and organization, while the nine gives wisdom with power drive through the five into the ones to create in and through the four.

The month 4.   The same figures are transposed to 11-4-1953. The chart shows the same positions, but the moral code and karmic lesson are changed to 2 and 6. The ones now rule the character, and the 4 adds practical ability in the form of adeptness, especially with the moral figure 2 from the day 11. The other figures do the same as before, but with determination as the ruling factor.

The years 4.   Same figures transposed to 11-3-1954. The chart again shows the same positions, but the strengths of the figures have been altered. The ones are the ruling factor. The 3 is now a force in the character and overrides the 4. The 4 has lost its ruling influence and gives way to the greater strengths of the ones and the 3. These examples are the positive aspect of the 4s. Let us now look at the negative aspect in the following examples.

The day 4.   4-4-1933 (moral code 4, karmic lesson 6). These 4s will control all that is done by this personality. The personality can and will be positive at times, but only when the inferiority can be set aside or forgotten in the excitement of doing or achieving something special, particularly if at work or in the home and then if they have a positive personality to work with, or from whom they will accept help and guidance.

The greatest difficulty with such a personality is the desire to do things their way regardless of help and suggestion. This is aggravated by the lack of the emotional expression figures which makes them shy and retiring. They cannot stand or put up with anyone standing looking over their shoulder or handing out free advice. They find this a problem even when employed and the boss stands over them and supervises their methods of doing things. They tend to do their best when left alone to do the job. The two 3s give them brains and artistic ability, but this would seldom be used in the positive sense. Being negative they would be finicky and fussy, lost in detail, with small things being of greater importance than the overall picture. The 9 would not help this personality because of the lack of joining figures, and when the karmic 6 became strong, mental stress would rob the personality of practical stability.

The month 4. 3-4-1943. The same figures transposed (moral code now 3, and karmic lesson 6). Now the 3 becomes the ruling figure and the 4 loses much of its power to influence. We have also lost the moral code 4, so we have lost the 4 influence to a moral code 3. This means that we cannot read the character as a 4 personality any longer. The 3s rule the character, and the 4s only give adaptability and the opportunity to do what the negative 3s decide.

The year 4. 3-3-1944. Once again the same figures transposed, but the moral code is now 3 and the karmic lesson 6. This is very much a 3 personality and the 4s are only an aid to the physical expression of the 3s.

The moral code depends how it is derived from the day figure. A day 4 moral code is to learn to control and rule attributes of the 4. A day 13 moral code is to create moral stability (4) to the physical, to control the mental power of the 3s down to physical level.

The above applies also to the karmic lessons to be learned from the total of the birth figures, 29-8-1965 = 40. So the karmic lesson is 4 and 0 for success with the karmic lesson. In the case of the karmic lesson producing the 0, this 0 will only work with the figure it started with, in this case the 4. In this case it means that the 4 will be learned properly and not halfheartedly.

NUMBER FIVE

POSITIVE FIVE

To be a positive 5 the personality needs to be born on the 5th or 15th day and have this figure backed up with positive 1s. Such a personality excels in positions where they can influence others by the spoken word—politicians, lawyers or salesmen/women.

They are fast, efficient workers, who constantly look for a new project to pit themselves against. Life to them is a challenge to be faced, then overcome or at least changed in some positive way. They have a calculating mind, which is factual and down to earth. The have the ability to mentally look into the future and see how they can organize self, others, and the circumstances to their mutual advantage.

Being very energetic and possessing great drive, they get things done by application of their personal effort. Control of energy gives them the personal ability to become very effective politicians, lawyers and sales people. This great personal energy and drive tends to make them impatient with those who cannot keep up with them in their chosen field of endeavour and they can be unkind with cutting and sarcastic remarks. If some other person is doing the chastising, they stick up for the underdog and insist that those who are not so well endowed be given a fair go. They are usually well adjusted and able to organize the environment so that it works for them. This ability to organize things is the natural rub off that comes with personal self-control and organization.

The 5 is ambitious and strives to get on, working hard for the good things in life. They are good providers for the family and are thoughtful and generous with employees who accomplish what they want done if they are speedy and accurate. A 5 will not tolerate poor workmanship and lazy people who try to take them down in any way. If not a strong motivating 5, they are sympathetic and kind and have a natural tendency to allow themselves to be led, for they tend to allow the heart to rule the head. They are fond of music and home life, but need to be looked up to and admired to be their most effective. They accept the truth that they are as good as they think they are. Devoted and protective of family, for they believe this to be their role, they chastise foolishness in privacy. Their power drive is usually pushed to the limit of their capacity and this uses up their reserve energy. They need Kali-phos, the biochemic remedy for mental fatigue to help restore the loss.

NEGATIVE FIVE

The negative 5 is a lover of change, simply because they hate the mundane. They are restless in their heart and mind thinking, having constantly a feeling of personal restriction. This is their major problem in life and the most difficult to overcome. They like argument for argument's sake and this keeps them unreliable and unpredictable. They literally think that change for the sake of change is a necessity of life.

While this instability can be advantageously used to develop the psychic abilities, it does nothing to help keep these abilities under control and reliable in their results. They seldom separate their own negative personality from the reality of the things they see or intuit.

Restlessness is the key to understanding this personality. They like to change jobs, places of living, the mind and heart thinking. They want personal freedom in all things, so dislike routine, but tend to force others to accept routine as necessary.

If the domestic scene is unsatisfactory, they seek consolation pleasure and sociability elsewhere. They can be emotionally and calculatingly obstinate and demanding, but they constantly fluctuate between this and being glib of tongue, having the persuasiveness of the con man. Because of an over-active imagination, aided by the natural intuition of the 5, they often become unintentional liars by deliberately concocting stories to suit their desires to build their own estimation of themselves. They ultimately come to believe their own fabrications. Methods such as Yoga, Astrology or Numerology help them to be as factual as possible.

They are often deliberately destructive with heart and mind when pessimistic; this causes them to be unpunctual and unreliable, also accident prone. They have a tendency to avoid any sort of personal responsibility and to blame others and life for things that go wrong. They have physical and mental dexterity and the energy to do, but are more often found organizing others to do what they should be doing for themselves. Pessimism develops acidity of the blood, and the taking of Kali-phos helps offset this problem; also, enough Epsom salts to cover a one-cent piece dissolved on the tongue once a day is a good remedy for over-acidity.

The positive 5 is easily seen when the personality is born on the 5th or 15th day and is supported with adequate positive ones. 5-11-1937 and 15-1-1973 are examples of the positive 5. The 5 is well backed up with positive ones, and the 3, 9 and 7 add to the strength and stability of the character by adding a figure in each corner of the chart. The day 5 with its moral code demands that the personality develop the characteristics of the 5 especially the intuitive aspect of the 5 so as to give greater pliability to the working side of the character. The 9 karmic lesson from the culmination of all the figures shows that this must be done with wisdom and insight. These two lessons show that the spirit of the personality is desirous of extending the natural ability of the 5 to be a balanced thinker with the ability to organize the things surrounding the personality and to learn to personally organize themselves in all they do. This of course develops the calculating aspect of the mind to find logical ways and means to accomplish the things which are uppermost in the heart and mind of the personality, without developing any of the negative aspects.

With the 15th day we find a distinct change comes over the 5 because of the change of the moral lesson of the day figure, which is of course now 6. While the chart shows the figures to be the same, the birth date does not; it must always be remembered that the position of the figures in the birth date controls the strength of the individual figures and consequently their ability to rule and guide the actions of the personality. This is also the reason why numerology works. It must be remembered that no matter what country or civilization the personality is born into, the day figure always carries the greatest strength. While alphabets change from country to country, and this has a distant effect upon the vibration of the name value, figures do not change and they are the universal language of the world and hold their value regardless of the language barrier.

The 15th day gives us a 6 moral code and this of course draws the personality towards the mental aspect of the character. So we would find this personality drawn to the more pure mental expression of the personality traits and the 9 would of course bring down wisdom to bear in the mental expression of the personality. On the psychic side, we would expect the intuition to become more acute in the mental field. A day figure 5 moral code would be drawn to more of the feeling expression.

The positive 5 is a personality well worth cultivating for the friendship they can and do give: factual, loyal and understanding in times of adversity.

The negative 5 is shown in two ways, but mainly with lack of positive ones to help the personality. The 5-5-1955, 5-11-1955, 5-1-1955, 15-5-1955, show no lack of ones, yet these personalities would find themselves in trouble because of the over abundance of 5s. The problem being that one 5 is good and adds beauty and strength, and if the personality has the positive ones as shown, seldom is any negativity developed with the addition of the moral code 5; but when we have two or more 5s plus a moral lesson 5, the problems of adversity, frustration and restlessness occur.

When there are more than two 5s, it will be found that the personality goes beyond the ability to make a critical appraisal of the situation and lapses into a state of personally criticizing anyone and everything, simply as a matter of course, and they must be helped to see what they are doing or lapsing into. Criticism for the sake of criticism is natural with these personalities and it is the duty of the numerologist to help this personality to see and overcome their tendency to fall into this trap of negativity, for there is no way that positive Karma can be achieved with a constant expression of criticism. Constant criticism and irritation is one of the major causes of cancer and kindred ailments.

Where the personality suffers from inferiority because of the lack of strong ones in the character, we have the same thing happening as above, but we have a weakness of purpose now. This shows up in the character as petty back-biting and ineffectual jealousy of why can't I do or have that, saying you aren't the only one who can do these things. They make a great show and fuss to try to get the attention of those around them, trying to prove that other people back them up in their protests, and that it is not fair that they be left out of sharing the good things of life that others have earned. They often lack the ability to do and achieve what the 5s are capable of.

Because the 5 is the center of the chart, it is called the figure of balance. It ties all the other figures together to form a freedom of expression so necessary in their world. It is the one figure that can and does overcome oral frustration more than any other figure. It is therefore in demand by those who have no middle figures.

NUMBER SIX

POSITIVE SIX

To be a positive 6, the personality needs to be born on the 6th, 16th, or 26th day.

The positive 6, unlike its negative counterpart, enhances every other figure in the character. It is a most advantageous figure, for it gives a face value, which is as it seems.

For people born on this day life is a well ordered plan. The 6 personality tackles life logically, so that each event will go in the direction desired. Careful planning is a must in lives with predetermined goals. The 6 is not infallible, but optimism gives positivity every opportunity to prove success. They like to experiment with life and situations. They also know that everything worth having in life and nature is more seldom achieved with haste as the driving factor.

The 6 personality is a thinker, quite often slow, but deliberate. They think with reason, and reason with their thinking. The 6 is the mental power of mind and opens the door to the realities of the heart and mind. Through the 7, this allows them to acquire new ideas; the 8, for control of the emotions with business-like acumen, also to know and experience love; then the 9, that inner wisdom that surmounts all, and to know even as he is known.

The 6 personalities have an analytical mind that like to delve deeper into life than is usual with most people. They are not afraid to seek and find the truth. They look for facts and figures to substantiate their inner ability to know and understand what they are looking at or assisting.

Love in the family has a deep sense of forbearance, for they love company and they give a great deal of loyalty to those they love, or are even only friends with. They love with the mind rather than the heart. Even though positive in thinking, the 6 tends to be slow and deliberate both in thought and action. A 2 speeds the thinking with quickness of movement. A 5 speeds with intuition. A 3 more towards the slow deep thinking. Ones, fours and sevens slow the active thinking.

NEGATIVE SIX

The negative 6 is a problem to its owner. Its worrying and constant inward fear aspect is bad for the nervous system; this causes ulcers, tumors, etc. It affects the nerves and the nerve tissue and the mylan sheathing surrounding the nerves, and through this the ability to maintain mental health. With strong 6s and a weak character it is certain that psychiatric care will be needed at some time, and possible several times in a lifetime.

The most obvious aspect of this is shown in the personality with moodiness, brooding and personal worry about self and work and family situations.

The depths of despair that the 6 can sink into has to be seen to be believed. They create their own problems as no other figure can. This is accentuated if coupled with 3s, 9s or both, but especially if there are two or more 6s in the chart.

Examples: 6-3-1969, or 3-9-1966, 3-3-1966, 6-3-1999. These figures lack determination or stability, also emotional expression figures. Mental insecurity through worry and introspection manifests in instability, and finally mental illness is the result. Also culmination figures do not help. The name needs to be a five. A stable home life is essential; also love with strong mental and emotional stability to the fore.

The negative 6 tends to be averse to any positive suggestions. They often have fixed minds, especially with 3s; open and vague minds with 9s. Because all these figures are on the top line, it is quite natural that illness and other problems will be of a mental nature. Also the thinking when negative will be channelled into escapism, not realizing or forgetting completely that only truth can set anyone free.

If not ill, they are argumentative and dogmatic. Seldom do they make friends, for they do not readily give genuine love.

Psychic abilities head into dark realms, and they cannot see that what they are seeing is only a feature of their own negative thinking. Possession by another spirit is possible but not likely. It is 99% fact that these personalities are possessed only by their own personal negative thinking.

The day figure of 6, 16 or 26 is naturally the strongest influence in the personality, and for the 6 to maintain a positive attitude it needs the help of positive ones, such as the 16 day or the 11 month. 6-11-1945, 16-11-1923, 26-11-1951. With the 6th of the 11th, even with the moral code of 6, the 1s, when backed up with the balance of the 5 and the physical stability of the 4, maintains good control over the positive thinking of the personality.

16-11-1923.   In this case the power of the 1s, to fix the mind and thinking on the constructive side of life, makes this person a brainy, clever thinker with a visual, intuitive perception which, if it gets the work to do, is capable of almost anything they wish to achieve through personal application. Normally in this situation of four ones, the character would tend to be pigheaded, but in this instance because of the power needed to control 6s and the 2, the control is much more malleable and not so rigid. With the moral code of 7 this person would excel in the business field. The bulldog determination with their ability to think in a situation would win more battles than they would lose. Even the culmination 6 would not upset these aspects sufficiently for this personality to become negative, except under extreme circumstances. The 1s give extreme control, and the 2 intuition, the 3 mental ability, the 6 a deep intuitive thinking, the 9 wisdom.

26-11-1957.   The 6 in this case is much more versatile, yet it is still a strong personality and a very capable one. The 1s give strong determination without obstinacy. The 2 is strong and therefore is more adaptable, and visual perception is better; the 5 gives balance coupling all the numbers together, and the 7 adds some get up and go with sacrifice for family.

6-6-1911.   The negative 6 is easily seen with the lack of positive 1s. It is obvious that, even with a 5 name, this personality is in trouble, for the lack of oral or emotional expression is a problem which sets the personality into a pattern which will be more than a little difficult to alter later in life. The three ones are too weak to help overcome the worry pattern, and as the moral and culmination 6s are added, the personality becomes more and more introspective, moody and broods. While there will be times of joy and happiness, this person will spend more time in seeking psychiatric help than they will developing their abilities to think, know or understand. Circumstances will govern their lives.

6-2-1954.   Being a strong 6 personality, but suffering from an inferiority complex, this person needs good positive and harmonious conditions if they are to rise above their natural lackadaisical attitude. They prefer others to take the reins and make their decisions, and with this personality this is the best thing for them. They have the ability to do the things positively if guided in the right manner and direction; especially if given loving incentive, they will support and follow their leader.

6-6-1966.   It will be obvious to the trained numerologist that this person is in trouble because of the excess 6s in the chart. The three obvious things are lack of strong ones, therefore inferiority complex, lack of emotional expression, the over-abundance of 6s which narrow the expressions and limit severely these expressions. It is possible with the overabundance of 6s this person may gain what would be regarded as an attitude of a moron, but this is because they themselves cannot cope with deep problems as they look within themselves. This person would find fear in their problem and would fear to face their own thoughts and feelings, and despair at not being able to cope with their thoughts. In some cases this could lead to insanity unless helped by the understanding of numerology.

6-5-1967.   This character, while being negative in the same sense of having an inferiority complex, would, if given the best circumstances of environment to live in, find the ability to offset the moodiness and broodiness of the 6s because of the aid of the stabilizing 5 and the acquiring of the 7. A name 3 would enhance the negativity with smallness and bigotry. A name 4 would help offset the introspection of the 6s, but would tend to make all the thinking become physically manifested in real illness. The 3 would be mental illness.

NUMBER SEVEN

POSITIVE SEVEN

The positive 7 is strong and reliable with the ability to accept themselves in the circumstances of life. When born on the 7th day, this personality tends to be shy and withdrawn. They like their own company, though not in a selfish way, and they do not like people who fuss or cause bother to others, for to them it could seem ostentatious, a showing off to get attention.

They like nothing better than to be alone with nature and their own personal thoughts, to some degree closed in but not negative. These personalities find deep peace among trees, ferns and creeks. They feel a deep sense of power with the restless moving sea. They like fellow human's company but they also enjoy solitude. They make wonderful trustworthy friends, but being secretive they find it difficult to share confidence with the average person and are only open within very close relationships. Positive 7s have the ability to go after and get what they want. They are quite possessive about the things they have acquired, and very possessively protective with loved ones.

Good artisans in their chosen field, they excel as accountants and research people. They enjoy the creating arts, writing and designing. They are strong personalities able to stand on their own merits, but they like to pit themselves against the power of the commercial world.

They are usually clever people, able to resolve the most difficult problems. The 7 is a strong reliable personality and the figure 7 is strong in its own right. It is so strong it is the one figure most able to change a negative one. They strive for perfection. They make good reliable partners both in business and marriage. They are sensitive to the needs of their spouse and their children, but tend to posses their family a little too much. This makes the family circle close and reliable through the love shared in the family. They are very spiritual, and make their spirituality live in their material living.

The speed of thinking and expression are governed by other figures. The positive 7's sensitivity makes them sensitive in different ways according to the other figures in the chart and the type of sensitivity can be gauged by other figures in the chart—mental, emotional, or physical or a combination of any of the figures.

NEGATIVE SEVEN

Born on this day, the power of the 7 takes the daydreaming capacity of the positive 7 into the negative of escapism, and the desire to run away from life. They like to get out of situations and usually perform tasks sulkily or with bad grace. They will do more work getting out of work than if they did it.

They tend to be old-fashioned and dogmatic, a real square, especially if drawn to physical expression, and are hard taskmasters in all situations.

The negative 7s are possessive and jealous to an extreme. They claim they are more sensitive to life than others, that they have more difficult lives than others. They can be bitter about what they believe is God's imposition upon them. The only truth in this is that their own negative attitude to life creates the problems they have to live through. Only truth can change this, for as you think in your own heart and mind, so you are, or become. There are no exceptions to this. The above is caused to some degree by the 7 having the power of the thinking Soul of humanity, for as the 1.2.3. represents the manifestation of God (i.e. 1. will; 2. love; 3. life,), so the 4.5.6. represents the manifestation of human into material experience, (i.e., 4. manifestation; 5.balance; 6.experimentation through the seeking mind), so does the 7.8.9. show humans' endeavour to attain oneness with itself (i.e., 7. lifting into spirituality; 8. through love; 9. into and through wisdom put into practice).

The 7 has to learn to sacrifice the negative for the joys and pleasures of the positive, instead of the usual sacrificing of the positivity to gain experience. The 7 has to learn that love cannot be possessed by possessing things, people or life. Love can only grow in a personality as the person tries to give it away. The more you give it away the bigger and better it grows. The negative 7 is demanding in its possessive self-seeking, and if physically inclined, sadistic in what it calls justice, especially if slighted or rejected. They hit back on a defensive attitude, such as: you did this to me, so take a dose of your own medicine. Defensiveness is a major key to this personality with their actions and reactions.

The positive 7 is shown in the same manner that most other figures are shown to be positive or negative. The day 7 is of course the strongest figure in the chart and is shown in samples 7-11-1956, 17-1-1956, 17-5-1961. With these three samples we see the positivity of the 7 change under the pressure of the position of the other figures. In the 7-11-1956 the 7 is made strong by the three ones especially by the month ones. The 5 adds balance and perseverance of purpose. The six gives a calculating mind of the 5 depth insight, which makes the personality sensitive through the 7's influence on the normal thinking of the character. The 7 gives the ability of foresight to the ones, to see and recognize the necessity of going after what is wanted, and getting results to the point of satisfaction. In the second example 17-1-1956, the ones are a little stronger in their action, and this makes the 7 even stronger in its normal action. The 5 and 6 have the same action. In the third example 17-5-1961, there is a reduction in power of the ones, so the personality will be a little more adaptable. The 5 gathers much more strength than in the other two examples. It adds more of the calculating action of the 5 to the person, and this hardens the attitude of the personality in its communication with others. This personality has more of the "what do I get out of it" attitude than the two others.

The 17-7-1941 is a very strong positive personality, but is operating on the physical level so the sensitivity of the 7 is of the physical kind, viz. they will feel the problems of others more than they would if they suffer the problem themselves. A cut finger in the family would cause this personality to have emotional physical cramps in stomach or chest in sympathy. The lack of emotional figures becomes a limiting factor in the life of this person, who will have a great deal of stress to overcome within the field of love and affection. A man would probably become overbearing and aggressive as the 8 gets built in, but would be a quiet possessive lover, needing to be loved very deeply. A woman would launch herself into the factor of a marriage but would find a lot of satisfaction crossed by deep hurts that will try the marriage to the fullest. Any negative outburst would be emotional, demanding and petulant. Loyalty would be of the demanding possessive kind needing reciprocation to be able to give of the love which must be developed. This personality needs a 5 name to develop and use the positivity to its best advantage.

The negative 7 is shown in the usual manner, either with an inferiority complex or an over-abundance of ones and/or zeros or an over abundance of 7s.

7-2-1922. This personality suffers from an inferiority complex and will have this all their life, but life is something which is to be changed and this is where the 7 shines, for it is the one number able to put the inferiority aside and bring the striving for ability to the surface. The inferiority of this personality is aided and enhanced by the over-adaptability of the 2s and this unsettled situation is a problem as this person also suffers from a lack of center numbers. The best help for this person is a three name, the culmination figure giving a 5. The moral code of 7 does not help, for the desire to have things their own way is reinforced as is the problem of sensitivity.

7-5-1975. The negative inferiority of this personality is compounded by the possessive selfishness of the 7s and the restless criticism contained in the 5s. The day and moral code 7s only highlight the fact that this personality will lead a very negative life of one problem after another, which will be created by the natural reaction of this personality to the circumstances of life, for they will see life and circumstance as their enemy. The reaction will be one of two ways, either taking on an outward aggressive appearance of a pseudo determination which would be defensiveness to attack life and circumstance, or will ultimately turn in on self and become a semi-invalid who will look to society for sustenance.

7-7-1977. This personality will be turned off. They will be quiet introspective and secretive. Because of lack of emotional figures, and also 6 and 4, this personality is divided. It is also limited by the overabundance of the 7s. Life is more difficult with these problems and this one will have to learn to sacrifice to the utmost of what they can understand and know about life.

Negative 7s usually have the desire to hoard things for a rainy day. While they will throw things away, they do not like doing so.

Positive or negative 7s can always pour out their heart and Soul in an artistic way, be it with music, painting, dancing or some other form of arty expression.

NUMBER EIGHT

POSITIVE EIGHT

The positive 8 is the figure of drive through the application of the desire to love what they are doing. The 8 produces personalities capable of organizing any parts of an enterprise into a successful cohesive whole.

Material success is important to the positive 8 and they need the emotional lift that the right kind of praise can give them. To succeed in anything, whether personal or the business field, it is necessary for them to be able to put their heart as well as their mind into the effort and situation.

While success is important, if there is not an admixture of their love, mind, and real self in what they are doing, they will never be satisfied with the result, and they will slowly but surely lose interest and drive in that particular project and will look for satisfaction elsewhere.

They usually have the ability to handle other's money and property with business-like acumen, but they are poor at handling their own as successfully. More often than not they allow the decisions of the heart to rule the head. They make friends easily, for they have a feeling of perception for the problems of others. They are tactful and gentle, but positive and forceful, yet they have quite a job restraining the irritation they feel, and this is often shown as emotional disappointment with the lack of consideration some individuals have for others. They have to learn to control the emotions with the mind. Though the 8 rails against the restraints of life, they usually accept them as necessary to the development of a better and more controlled nature.

The 8 has to learn it is the love it seeks; it has to learn that the only love it can have is the love it gives away, for as it experiences the love it is giving away, it keeps the love it is experiencing for itself. It has to learn that the secret of loving is the sharing of the experience of loving.

NEGATIVE EIGHT

The negative 8, being utterly opposite to the positive 8, reaches down into the depths of despair and negativity that stops them from believing in the positive side of life. Because aggressiveness is the opposite of inferiority it is used as a tool of the negative 8 to impress others with a positivity it does not possess. This is often mistaken for the real determination, which of course it is not, for it is emotional aggressiveness. This is easily seen in reactions of the personality who, lacking a calculating mind of wisdom, says, "I can do it even if you can't." The aggressive drive rails against restriction and shows that the heart and the emotional thinking rules the action in any situation. The mind is the servant of the emotions.

They do not realize, as the positive 8 does, that the way of victory over the self and the world is more often achieved by the flexibility to bend before the onslaught of stress and strain; then, with strength and courage, apply the gentle vigor that achieves with an active will—the power that utilizes the correct emotional drive.

Negative 8s, if coupled with 2s, shows them to be very emotional even though they have mental balance. They are often sorry for themselves. Emotional reaction robs them of energy and they are often nerve debilitated. They are feeling psychics with abilities that are more hindrance than help, for they take on the sickness or the troubles of others, then live them as their own.

The injection of their negativity makes them very unreliable as a psychic. Negative 8s claim they are too sensitive to be able to resist the evil of others, which is incorrect as they are only reacting to a situation of circumstance with their own negativity.

Being very sensual they often give way to passions, both in sex and anger. Anger is either hot and unreasonably passionate or cold-blooded, calculating, cruel and sadistic. A restless nature, they like travel, or they dig their own little hole to live in. Fear is a problem, and can be unreasoning, also defensive. It causes them to act in impulsive ways which can be quite unpredictable.

The positive 8 is shown in the usual way of being a day figure assisted by positive ones. A very positive 8 is as follows: 8-12-1954. This personality is an emotionally oriented personality which is shown by the 8 and the 2 being very strong and the 5 giving support to the emotional expression. The two 1s give strength of determination to the emotional drive of the 8. The 4 gives practicality to the physical actions with adaptability and skill. The 2 gives creative ability. The 5, calculating inquisitive mind assisted by a natural intuition. The 8 gives a positive feeling E.S.P. ability. This personality is activated by a highly sensitive E.S.P. awareness, which gives it a mental ability much to be admired. This personality could develop a good x-ray diagnostic ability, in other words it has the ability to see the aura and to communicate with the so-called dead.

A personality having an extra 1 such as 18-12-1954 would be as above, but would lack a little of the high sensitivity of the E.S.P. facilities. These are lessened by the addition of the 1 which adds greater determination but tends to give a little more rigidity to the personality, and thus inhibits some of the E.S.P. faculties. This rigidity gives a greater sense of orthodox brain power rather than psychic ability.

A month 8 can be very strong when assisted by very positive ones: 11-8-1965. The three ones really turn this personality into a one personality, nevertheless the 8 is very strong in this instance. The 8 gives to this personality a deep strong need to love others, but could eventually turn off if reciprocation is not enough to meet the needs of the heart and mind; for one of the greatest needs of this personality is to love deeply, passionately and strongly, and to have a visible and audible reciprocation. This applies to the business field as well as the social. This love aspect applies to all positive 8 charts.

If we have no 8s in the chart, but we have a moral code 8, then the personality has come to add this type of loving to the character. The success attained in this area will depend on the figure traits the personality has chosen to take on in this life.

NOTE: It is the spirit of the personality which chooses the character, and even the type of body it wants to use. The only inherited aspects it finishes up with is the color of hair, eyes, teeth, skin, etc., which is given by the natural lineage of the parents. Other influences include the environment the parents supply, and the impingement of the personality characteristics which the parents naturally use to train the child in their way of life while it is growing and developing its own personality strengths and weaknesses.

Negative 8 is shown in the usual manner of only one 1 giving the personality an inferiority complex, with the 8 bringing out the aggressiveness of the 8 to compensate for the lack of determination.

8-2-1934.   The 1 equals inferiority complex and lack of persistence. The 2 adaptability and instability in emotional situations. The 3 clever mind is more often wasted in the negative situations by the fastening on the small details and being demanding of super accuracy. The 4 helps practicability when inferiority is put aside. The 8 desires love, but doesn't know how to get it, so frustration reverts to aggressiveness instead of power drive. The 9 seldom gives the wise help it is capable of, especially with the karmic lesson of 9 causing negativity as does the moral code of 8.

A personality having a birth date of 8-8-1988 is in great difficulty. This is easily seen by the limiting factor of the over abundance of the 8s. Also the division caused by the lack of 4, 5, 6, and of course the personality has only one 1, and this brings out the usual problems of inferiority and over-aggressiveness caused by too many 8s. The 9 is not helpful as it is over-ridden by the 8s. The karmic lesson 6 tends to accentuate the negativity. The 6 with its introspective tendency, causes this personality to be very emotionally and mentally sensitive. This brings out the mental cruelty of the 8s, especially when the personality cannot cope with their own personal problems. They take up a defensive attitude, and this makes them hit back at other people and things through their reaction to the situation. They are, or can be cruel in thought, word, and deed. The mental becomes cold-blooded and calculatingly sadistic. They enjoy their sadism for the time it occurs, even though they know it is wrong. When in this state of mind they do not worry about the damage they cause to others. There is no way the 8 can do any of these things without consciously knowing and being fully aware of what they are doing.

NUMBER NINE

POSITIVE NINE

The positive 9 is shown in the usual manner, the day or month figure backed up by positive ones. If born on this day of the month, this personality is usually attuned to the Soul of humanity and to the deeper rules of life, which govern, influence and affect all lives.

The 9 has good outer wisdom, but is happiest when expounding upon the deep inner knowledge of life. The 9 has a wide, understanding mind; while deploring narrowness and bigotry, still manages to be surprised, but not shocked at, the stupidity of the actions of some individuals and groups. They have a mind which is a channel to the mystical inner life of humanity, but it needs positive control to be its most effective. As a personality, the 9 lives to the highest of ideals, for it is the vehicle of the inner wisdom and does things because it is right to do so. It is the channel for discovering the deep hidden knowledge in the computer mind of God. The 9 desires to love for the sake of loving.

The positive 9 likes to obey the law, for it sees the law working in all life. These people find fulfilment in truth and honesty. They are drawn to the church and church work, but find their true fulfilment when they work and create within the heart of the community. They live best when giving of their talents in a spirit of service to the community as a whole. They love people and life.

They love travel and a changing environment that opens new vistas which teach of the depth and beauty of life. If aided by a positive 6 or 3, they can delve into the seamy side of life for the experience that enables them to know and understand the problems which other people suffer.

From an esoteric point of view and looking into the very far and distant future development of humanity, the 9 is the last step in the chain of life. This does not mean that because a personality is learning the moral code of the 9 that it is their last incarnation. It would not be common sense to think so, for the facets of the 9 which have to be learned to completely round out the beauty of the 9 takes countless numbers of lives. In the same way, it is not wisdom to think of any one of us as young or old Souls. What we are seeing is only the attitudes of the personality framework which is being used to learn specific lessons (another day in school of the education of the Soul). All evidence points to the fact that most of us could be classed as middle-aged Souls.

The 9 symbolizes true wisdom through right personal loving of humanity; it is the true path for all life to follow and is even higher than love. It is the ultimate of all life to be attained through the wheel of birth and death. 9s are unselfish, loving and sacrificial, having an adaptable nature which is often too sensitive to human suffering. The 9 aids the psychic's need for truth. Law and teaching are the vocations rather than business.

NEGATIVE NINE

The negative 9 is more of a problem to itself than to others, for born on this day this personality can be explosive, both in love and bad temper. Their emotions are not stable. They tend to be selfish, domineering and aggressive, or they are the complete opposite—meek and mild almost without a mind of their own. They lack the will to live up to the responsibility of life and to the fullness of their nature.

They tend to criticize petulantly and they fail to be positive in so many ways, especially if they do not get the accolades they think they deserve for the fiddlingly small efforts they make on behalf of others. They can be wearisome and dragging on those they live with.

As personalities they seldom accept the responsibilities of marriage and shy away from anything that causes them pain, particularly childbirth. If sex does not satisfy in the early experiments, they turn off and become unsatisfactory partners. They blame the partner and God for all their troubles yet it is they who lack the ability to adjust to love and employment and they let everything irk and irritate them. Through this they often develop psychosomatic illnesses such as headaches, neuralgia, rheumatism, arthritis, asthma, ulcers, migraine and mental traumas, especially when coupled with 6s or 3s. They are unable to stick to their word for they cannot see a real need for their word to be their bond. They are unable to concentrate for very long, and they lack personal self-control and can see no reason to do anything about it. Craving love, they are often frustrated, then tend to be over-bearing and emotionally pigheaded.

9-11-1954. This example of the positive 9 shows the great wisdom of the 9 in action, for the chart shows that this personality has come to bring the natural wisdom down to earth in the most practical and spiritual way. The three ones give strength to the personality for control over the over-abundance of 9s, and set the pattern for the rest of the life. Though the 5 and 4 are not strongly positioned, they gather strength from their natural action within the character and from the action of the ones. The 4 adds practical skill and adeptness to the ones and the 5 adds the balance that comes with a calculating mind. The 5 also heightens the inner perceptivity of the 9s and helps to build a firm channel for the flow of the excess of the wisdom this person is capable of tapping into. This personality will develop a good, accurate and clever mind particularly if the environment allows them to use their talents effectively for the good of others.

19-11-1975 would be a good positive 9 personality. The difference in the action would come through the 7 in the chart. This adds greater strength to the character, also a deeper sensitivity for the 7 heightens the personality's feeling for others. This has to be learned and directed into a very positive activity to obtain the best from the personality. The 1 and 0 of the day moral code of course adds greater strength to the whole personality, especially around the 19th birthday year. The karmic lesson 7 gives greater strength to the sensitivity, but adds strength and reliability to the character.

10-9-1945 or 11-9-1957 are good examples of the positive 9 personality. In these charts the personality has less problems in the mental area, for the flow of wisdom through the 9s is easier to control and there are no extra 9s from the moral or karmic lessons.

When the 9s are in the year or century figures, they cannot be called a 9 personality, but if there are three 9s such as 11-5-1999, the 9s will have a strong influence on the rest of the character, but this will be offset to some degree by the building in of the moral and karmic lessons.

The negative aspects of any figure are of course the problem of lack of determination and persistence to succeed in getting positively aimed results. Inferiority does not have determination or persistence, and the lack of these factors results in a lack of positive drive, or it could cause the personality to be over-aggressive to prove they do not have an inferiority complex. If we have an overabundance of 9s, this narrows their capabilities of expression and, as this is limitation, this is also negative.

9-9-1999 is a classic example of all the above showing inferiority complex which no doubt the personality would at times try to offset with vigorous displays of so called determination, but which would really be aggressiveness to cover their weakness This would be short-lived and very soon the character would drop back to the meek, shy and mild person they really are.

The over-abundance of 9s opens the channel of wisdom and knowledge too wide for such a meek and mild personality. This makes them too sensitive to all the negative aspects of reaction like hurt, pain, knock-backs etc., for the desire of this type of person is to be loved rather than to love.

This personality is introverted as shown by the lack of emotional expression figures; they are unable to get the deep inner self out to others. They are shy and reserved, with a secretive nature. These aspects do nothing to help the determination of positivity, so these people are more than 50% of their time in a negative phase.

While negatively expressing personalities not only find it difficult to get through life without considerable help from others, it must be remembered that we all have come here to learn with and through the personality we have chosen. Karma, or as we Christians say, "AS YOU SOW, SO SHALL YOU REAP," has a major role to play in our choosing.

ZERO

The 0 is a very important figure, yet many numerologists ignore this important feature. Imagine leaving the 0s out of a date such as 10-10-1990. Such an act would quite possibly take your basic incarnating spirit into the next governing ray period as we have seen before from our ray chart, and this would of course have far different energies affecting the incarnating personality.

When born on the 10th, 19th or 28th of the month, each of these dates reduce to the moral code of 10 or 1 and 0. The 1 and 0 as a moral code figure must be read in unison with each other, and the 0 in the moral code lesson cannot affect the other figures in the character reading. A moral code culmination can only affect the numbers creating the moral code, i.e. in 19-12-1946, the moral code of 10 would only affect the 19 and must be read in conjunction with them.

When the 0 is part of the birthday figures as in 20-10-1960, the 0 affects all the other figures in the birth date, and this is in effect all the time.

Personalities born with 0s in their birth date are people who can be one-pointed in going after and obtaining the objective they decided to aim for. They can weld the heart and mind into a single desire and hence single idea. This means they have a strong determination to succeed all of the time; whereas the culmination figure 0 shows they have to learn to marry the mind and heart into one idea. It can be said without fear that where there are 0s in the personality, this personality will succeed in whatever they desire to do or achieve.

Born on the 10 or 19 day, the personality is already a determined person, so the culmination 10 enhances the determination of the character. The 1 of the 10 gives determination and the 0 success. While the 1 of the 19 day character is strong determination, the 1 is tempered by the wisdom of the 9. The 28 is of course emotionally inclined, the 2 and 8 gives emotional energy and drive, therefore the sum of the 2 and 8 figures = 10 becomes necessary for stability and learning to use the energy and drive to succeed when the heart and mind desire the one thing.

28-4-1906: These figures show an inferiority, but success should be assured because of the 0 and the confidence boosting moral code 10. 5-8-1960 shows the same inferiority, but it is more severe with the calculating 5 and 8 both in the emotional field. 3-6-1970, is mentally orientated, quiet, reserved, but with potential to succeed. 28-10-1970 has emotional energy and drive, success is assured. 28-1-1930, success is also assured through the emotional and mental drive.

NEGATIVE ZERO

The negative 0 is easily seen with the usual inferiority complex lacking ones, or an over-abundance of 1s or 0s. The over-abundance of 1s or 0s makes the personality too rigid with obstinacy. This is of course is one of the most prominent aspects of the 0 negativity. This can be also seen with the negative emotional and mental figures. This is a little more difficult to interpret than the straight out figures, but it will be achieved with practice. An over-abundance of 0s points to habitually dominant characters, who tend to lose the ability to think clearly and precisely as does the normally determined 1 personality.

They are domineering and irritable when things do not go the way they have planned, for frustration sets in, and this causes an overbearing attitude in the general outlook and expression.

It is amazing but true that a 0 personality can also give up and lack the initiative to make a decision. This usually shows a defeated person, without the will to do more than just exist.

When born on the 10, 19 and there are several 1s in the figures, these personalities will make a great showing of their determination. This shows, through their expression of thought and action, these extremes simply revealing the limitations of their character. Their field is so narrow they will have a black and white nature. They demand facts that are see-able, touchable and provable to the senses. The mind will be closed to the abstract, or anything that cannot be seen with the naked eye. If born on the 28 day, they use their will with the emotions uppermost. They can literally be ruled by stupid, dogmatic, emotional thinking, and will often be heard to say, "I know what I am talking about and you cannot prove it wrong." With E.S.P. abilities they either believe they are all knowing, or they become so afraid of what they are and what they see, that they turn off, and assign everything to our orthodox devil. To change their mind on anything, one must plant a thought and let it grow.

It is almost impossible to have a negative 0 even with an inferiority complex, for the 0 is constantly trying to offset the inferiority, nevertheless it is true that the personality will have an inferiority complex and this will be for all their life. If the 0 had the backing of the other figures it will have the ability to override the inferiority and succeed in positive activity. If it does not have the aid of other figures, then the 0 will give success to the personality to be a failure. In such a case the numerologist must be reminded it is the spirit who has chosen the personality with which to learn the lessons it needs to know. This is chosen with the view of Karma to reap what we have sown. This of course means that reincarnation is a must and the lessons are learned life after life.

The numerologist must take into account all this and still endeavour to help and aid the personality to be as positive as possible; after all, as the Christian world says, "We are our brother's keeper."

The real limitations of the 0 shows up in the over-abundance of itself, for three or more 0s does the same as any other figure—it narrows the thinking and acting of the personality to the point where it is too obstinate and/or domineering etc. These examples, 10-10-1900, or 20-

10-2000, or 30-10-1930, show much limitation of personal expression simply because it narrows the field or participation in physical life.

10-10-1900 has lessons of 10 and 3. These lessons do not help this personality. The 1 and 0 only make the personality even more rigid. The 3 then becomes a negative aspect with the limitation of the 3 being uppermost. A 5 name is a must if any help is to be given to this person.

With the 20-10-2000, the 2s are a hindrance because of the division caused by the lack of 4,5,6, and of 3,5,7. The inferiority 1 will either be very bad or so adamant with the 0s that the personality will be difficult to cope with. Once again a five name is a must for this situation.

THE POSITIVE ZERO

The positive 0 is seen when there is one 0, or a maximum of two 0s in the chart. Three 0s or more in the chart shows the normal effect of limitations that come from an over-abundance of any one figure.

The 10-5-1937 is a perfect example of a very good positive 0. This 0 has the power necessary to weld this personality into the balanced and stable thinking machine that it is. This person has all the attributes of character that enables them to be practical, down to earth, and yet retain and use a very high degree of spirituality. The 1s give positive drive and initiative with a naturally good persistence to succeed at what is initiated. The 7 gives the practical go after and get, to possess, and with the ability to sacrifice those things of the heart and mind necessary to obtain a better result, or a better goal. The 5 gives the balanced, calculating thinking mind the ability to organize self and the events and circumstances around them. The 5 supplies that intuitive perception which aids the 3 to make the most of its accurate mental capabilities. The 3 through the 5 and into the 7 builds the practical outlet for the spirituality of this personality to show itself in the material scene. The 9 gives wisdom which can be drawn upon by the rest of the character in all it does. The 0 gives the cementing ability of the 0 to succeed in what the heart and mind most desires. The moral code lesson of 10 makes this personality even stronger in its positivity, though a tendency to pedantic obstinacy could be a problem at times. The culmination of 8 enhances the character through the 8's personally applied drive, especially with love as the motivating factor.

The name could be almost any vibration without real detriment to the character's operation, but a 2 or 4 name would give the best pliability and activation.

The following sets of figures would be a good indication of positive 0 values.

20-10-1965, 30-1-1970, 31-10-1970, 1-10-1970, 1-10-1935, 1-10-1938. There are a good many combinations from which spirit can choose a positive 0 personality.

Unlike the other figures which have the ability to work on their own as the individual figures they are, the 0 can only work in combination with another figure. We cannot have a 0 day or month or century, but we can have a 0 year.

MASTER NUMBERS

NUMBERS ELEVEN AND TWENTY-TWO

Much has been said and done by numerologists about the over-emphasizing of esoteric aspects of 11 and 22 numbers. These aspects do exist in the 11 and 22, but the over-emphasis of the importance of these numbers does not allow the inexperienced numerologist the ability to read the numbers exactly.

Number Eleven

In the case of the 11 day, we have two very strong ones. This of course is very good for the drive and determination, while the moral code of 2 adds a visually creative, inspirational aspect to the eleven, hence the reason for their keenness to over emphasize the importance of the 11.

The number 11 is called a master figure for it brings the inspiration and power of the 2 to the character (see below). For the 11 to be a master figure the person must be born on the 11th day of the month. No other day gives the master number despite what some books say. It is easily seen if you read the 11 with its culmination of 2, that the inspirational and creative aspect of the 2 will show in the character, and the ages of 11 and 20 will show an emphasizing of these characteristics. The person will have built in the tendencies of the 2 by the age of 20, and thereafter will be putting into effect the practice of what they have learned about the 2. The 1s of the day 11 give determination and strength to the mastering of the aspects of the 2s as well as the rest of the character. Almost the only way the 11 can be negative is to have too many ones. This will mean the 2 cannot break through the narrow-mindedness of the ones.

Number Twenty-Two

In nearly every case the day 22 is more hindrance than help. Remember the fact that 2s need very positive 1s to help them from slipping into inferiority complexes. The moral code lesson 4 from these 2s shows the 22 is seldom in control of itself. They have to learn to get their feet on the ground and keep them there, or there can be no mastery of the potential power aspects of the two 2s. It is greatly desirable to have a 7 somewhere in the chart with these 22s to allow the personality to overcome the inferiority generated by the 22s overpowering positivity absorbing aspects.

With people who use the so called master figure to impress others with their mystical powers, all I can say is they could use their skills in a more practical way to help others, like actually developing these powers properly.

KARMIC NUMBER

This number, not coinciding with the time of death, is when the personality is more developed and will learn on the astral much better. The more esoterically backward the person, the more likely they are to see out the full term of their life. Example: 29-8-1974 = 40 = 4. The figure 4 shows that the time allotted for the karmic lessons is to the age of 40. Another example is 15-3-1952 = 26 = 8, therefore 80 is the expected life span for their lesson to be learned.

There are cases however where an entity is quite advanced, and after completing their Karma allotted for this life, can then take on another lot of Karma in the one life. This is possible if that entity has thoroughly learned its set lesson for this incarnation. This of course will eliminate the need for at least one future life when they are nearing the end of their incarnations. This will only apply to a few people advanced beyond the normal level. It has been known that there are even cases where an entity has taken on a third lot of Karma, but this will apply to even fewer of the populace, and I doubt that I shall reach too many of these people with this book. I imagine they will indeed be a rare breed at this stage of evolution. Of course in the future where humanity will be becoming more and more developed, this will then be more common. Just because a person lives past the age where their Karmic lesson has been completed does not mean that they are in immanent danger of dying. As we advance, many of us of humanity need the extra time to digest the finer points of the more complicated lessons. Just like our normal school, the lessons get more complicated each year, so do our life lessons get more complicated as we climb the ladder of evolution.

MORAL CODE AND KARMA

The moral code comes about by adding all the numbers of the day figure, e.g., 13-6-1956—the moral code would be 4 which would be the day figure 1 and 3 added together. This moral code is a primary karmic lesson to be learned. This lesson is obviously meaning that the 4 must learn to control the power of the three in the day figure within the physical level.

The other karmic lesson is derived by adding all the number in the birth date arriving at 13-6-1956 = 31 = 4 which gives a karmic lesson of 4. The difference between Karmic lessons and moral code is to understand one is from the day and one is from the total date. The definitions are simply to designate between the two, as both are karmic requirements.

You will notice in this instance that both the numbers come to 4. In such a case as this, both lessons having the same number indicates that the personality did NOT learn their past life lessons satisfactorily; therefore they have to take on the lesson again in this life.

The wise people who read numerology and have this occur to them will take note that if this is not addressed and the lessons learned, then in the not too distant future a life will occur where the person will be a paraplegic, and they will have less physical time and more time to think on their lessons. If once again they refuse to learn their lessons, the next life will be that of a quadriplegic, and they will have even more mental time than physical; and finally, if they again do not heed this lesson, in the future life they will be in a coma until they learn their lessons. If they still refuse they will keep leading lives of coma until they do learn their lessons. Once the lesson is learned the coma victim either dies or recovers from the coma. Any of these conditions naturally has a physical trigger, but the reason and the outcome is the same.

When looking at the karmic numbers, one can usually tell when the personality starts to accept the lesson. With the karmic number of 4, the lesson should be learned by the age of 40, just as the 6 will be learned by the age of 60. We will deal with the karmic 6 number to just grab at one number at random, but here we must realize that we must use the perfect number to calculate this, and this perfect number is 9.

Nine, being the perfect number, means that you can add many numbers together and 9 will make no difference. To try this, take as many numbers as you wish and add them together.

Example: $3+4+7+8+1+5+7=35=8$

Now use the same numbers and put some 9s in it no matter how many you use.

$3+4+9+7+8+1+9+5+7+9=62=8$

Make up some numbers for yourselves and try this, and you will find your own proof of this, that nine is indeed the perfect number.

You will see that the nines make not the slightest difference in the outcome when reduced to the lowest figures.

Let us get back to our number 6. We keep adding 9s to this number … 15-24-33-42-51-60. You will see there is a point where the numbers reverse. This is the age where the personality turns their thinking around to start their karmic lessons (give or take a couple of years). There is a definite change in thinking at this age. Check this out on yourself. This is the same for the moral code and the karmic number equally.

The Karmic and moral code lessons are represented by the same basic meanings of the numbers involved. This should be better understood now that all the numbers have been dealt with fully and you have well and truly mastered the number's meaning.

So we now proceed to the revelation of which psychic center we enter and leave our bodies during our sleeping hours.

These centers often erroneously called "chakras" by most people are the energy points of our bodies. Firstly a chakra and center are not the same things. Chakra extends only to the etheric level, whereas the center extends to the highest level.

To understand this we must go to the basics of the centers and see their development. There are nine centers, and these are Crown, Third eye, Throat, Heart, Solar Plexus, Navel, Genital, Base and Aura. The human body automatically enlivens these centers at a certain time in the age of the body.

Promptly at five years the crown center opens, at six the third eye, at seven the throat, eight the heart, nine the solar plexus, ten the navel, eleven the genital, twelve the base, thirteen the aura, and then all the centers are opened which occurs at the age of thirteen. The old Jewish scholars knew this, as a child became an adult at the age of thirteen for the reason that this is when all the centers are in play, hence the original reason for the Jewish Bar Mitzvah.

If one adds all the numbers of the birth date and gets them down to the lowest number, these will equate to the age of the center that is the entry and exit center of the body. All answers must then come down to numbers between 5 and thirteen. If the number comes to under five, say a 4, then that number will be $1+3=4$, or if a 3, it will be $1+2=3$, or $1+1=2$.

Therefore if one's birthday is $22-7-1956=32=5$ which would be the crown center, or if the date was $21-6-1965=31=4$ which must be one and a three giving 13, then the center would be the aura because the Aura has the 13-pointed star or lotus petals.

These centers must be protected from damage if at all possible. Of course the only way the aura can be damaged is from excess addictions of alcohol, drugs or some other psychic way. This will damage the auric field by tearing what is called the nepenthe veil, giving a permanent problem of what is commonly called by alcoholics the Delirium Tremens, or the popular name of the DTs, where one sees all sorts of horrid visions.

THE SUFI NUMBER

If you examine the Sufi tradition, the numerology will also tell you which number you are. Old Sufi tradition tells us we have a basic character number, which also affects our character. While this is true, it will not affect the normal reading of your personality with this system, but if you want your Sufi number from this system, then add the day and month figure and bring it to the number within the 5 to 13 range as with the system of the center for entering and exiting your body during sleep.

As with the entry and exit center, we then count the center that is in sympathy with the number of petals.

Example: If the number finished up 2, we must go to $1+1=2$, therefore the center would be 11. The 11-petal center would be the genital center which is the 7th center, therefore your Sufi tradition number would be 7.

Let us now have a few dates to practice on.

First Example: 11-11-1971

9 (2) 111111 (4)(4) 7 (numbers in brackets 2 = moral code, number 4 = karmic number, number 4 = name).

We look with sadness at this numerology, but this is the lesson that this Soul has taken upon itself to learn in this life. This lesson would indeed make this person very hard to live with, but I reiterate this is the lesson this personality has chosen to rise above. The six ones show too much positivity and you can see instantly that the personality is very narrow minded and bigoted and very aggressive, with their view being the only one that could possibly be right in that personality's opinion. The attention to their personal occupation would be very dogged and determined, and said person would demand accuracy of themself as well as others around them. All actions in life would be an outlet of self expression and very important to this person. We also see the frustration gaps produced by the lack of 2.5.8

and 4.5.6. We interpret this as Schizophrenia because of the lack of 4.5.6., and certainly lack of emotional expression with the lack of 2.5.8. Because of this the personal thoughts deep within the emotional self would be kept private, and rarely would any other person know what lurked in the mind or what is deep within the emotional self. These would be kept secret from all except for a very special few. The moral code is 2 and the Karmic number is 4. This means that this person is obviously to learn how to make themself more flexible (2) and to use this flexibility on their physical level(4). This would be a very hard lesson to rise above with such numerology, but the Soul has its reasons for dishing out such a lesson. For Clarity the Moral code, karmic number and name number are written within Brackets.

The lack of emotional expression (shown by the lack of 2.5.8.) also indicates that a person with such an emotional lesson nearly always loves to float in water by swimming or bathing. Note that the emotional figures are also the figures for the element water. Floating signifies the emotional urge to float in the mind and emotions upon the astral level. It is literally the physical way of day dreaming.

The lack of 4.5.6. here (being on the earth line) also points out that they would very likely benefit from the soothing effect of gardening, or somehow being in physical touch with the soil, like walking barefoot in the gardens.

The name in this example also comes to a 4 which is most unhelpful in any way. A five name here would certainly be much more desirable.

I have noted that a huge number of the better class of actors and actresses and politicians showing above normal ability have a tendency towards schizophrenia. This allows them to really live the role they step into when they are performing. One could say that in this occupation, Schizophrenia can be a real advantage. Another place where schizophrenia is an advantage is an organist where it is necessary to have complete independence of each hand and each foot. The seven shows the ability to go after and get what is wanted. The seven also shows that when this person is very calm, they person would love to be in a family situation caring for those classed as their immediate family, but when angered or in defense of family, they would defend their family with any means necessary no matter how nasty a level must be sunk to, to get the job done. To them the ends would justify the means. The extreme positivity shows a seven trait that is self reliance, but still showing great caring for the brood. Certainly not a parent to be trifled with, and if you dare to threaten her offspring, you do so at your own peril.

Second Example

3 6(6) 5 (8) 1 4 7 Take Michaelangelo 6-3-1475 (bracketed numbers: 6 = moral code, 8 = karmic number).

The first thing noticed is that he had a bad inferiority complex with low self-esteem, but secretly wishing to be admired and recognized. Despite any outward appearance, he would be a worrier and he would be always striving to improve himself, thinking his next work MUST be better than the last. He would check out every detail before he put it into action, and then re-check to ensure he had it right. He had the mind of a modern computer, fast, accurate, and visionary due to the psychic ability of his three and seven. The three and seven also supplied him with an abundance of artistic talent, and this would show in many fields. The four allowed him to manifest his ideas and work down into the physical thereby producing some of the world's best and enduring artworks. The 1.4.7 gave him the physical dexterity to accomplish practical deeds, while the 3.6. gave him the mental ability to see his finished article in his mind before he even started it. With the five it is a foregone conclusion that he would be able to couple the physical and mental together to produce the treasures he left for humanity.

Because he was in actual fact a negative personality, the three would ensure he was always looking for the pat on the head telling him he was a good boy, and had done good work. The seven denotes that he would be a hoarder of all sorts of bits and pieces, saving them for a rainy day. The 5 would make him rather restless and he would be anxious to finish his project to start the next. He would struggle with this urge and would have to control himself or he would have much unfinished work.

His visions and voices would plague him all his life unless he understood he was a very psychic individual. This is most unlikely, for in those days he would have been burnt at the stake for witchcraft if he mentioned this fact. We can see his moral code was 6 and his karmic number was 8, telling us he had the lesson in this life of learning to reason with love and intuition. He entered his body during sleep via his heart center, therefore this must be the sensitive area and protected during this lifetime. Not knowing exactly what his friends called him, the name would be irrelevant here unless we could find that out. I doubt they called him Michael, maybe Mike, Mick, Kel, but without the popular name I could not give the proper effect of the name. In any case the name is always the weakest number in the chart. In spite of the name number being weak, it still does let an energy flow through the chart.

A third example: 20-2-1950 (moral code=2, karmic number =19=10).

Here we see that an inferiority complex is present. This is quite evident because of the lack of any positive 1s. The only one present is a century 1 and that of course is a weak 1, and we know from our dealing with the 2s that we need very strong 1s to overcome the energy of the 2s. This personality would therefore be a negative 2 personality, but remember, any one can be positive without any sort of stress or pressure.

This makes the personality very meek and mild normally, and allowing others to walk over them unless they make an effort to assert themselves. This however would be quite an effort, but they can achieve it all the same. If riled enough, they can respond with a bout of anger which will surprise all their friends, but just as quickly lose this anger again, returning to the meek-mannered person they really are.

The two 2s make this person very adaptable and flexible in all aspects, and able to bring down ideas, but putting them into practice would be rather slow, deliberate, and careful because of the lack of physical numbers. This can make them very good artists because they are slow and sure of getting things right.

The 5 would indicate that the clairvoyant ability of the 2 would also be reinforced by the 5s clairaudience, and the spirituality of the 9. With the lack of good, positive physical numbers this person would be a daydreamer at times, letting all sorts of ideas run rampant through the mind. This daydreaming is actually the clairvoyant mind working to bring a coupling of thoughts from the physical to the higher realms, and vice versa.

The 5 would also make the person restless and wanting to always keep new ideas flowing to satisfy that restlessness. If this cannot be achieved, then that person would get itchy feet and want to travel around a lot.

Very flexible in manner, this person could mix with anybody and change their nature to suit the surrounds and people.

They are rather fickle in many ways, unless they meet "the person" they are suited to. They soon tire of fools and don't suffer them gladly most of the time.

This person seldom ever wants to be top dog in anything, but will accept the post if it is put on them, but they prefer to remain no higher than 2nd fiddle in the scheme of things.

The Moral code of $2+0$ shows that they are learning the lesson of the 2, and they are determined to succeed is shown by the 0 in the moral code. The Karmic number 1 shows that they will be very determined to gain positivity, and the 0 shows that they will be very slow and deliberate, pushing forward with their goal if they believe they know exactly what their goal is. This positivity is a very gentle push, not a violent shove, but this person will push relentlessly until their goal is reached

$20+2+1950=37=10$ shows the number of lotus petals in the center that they enter and leave the body. This of course equated to 6, and the navel center is of course the 6th center.

A good exercise here is to see how many other features you can dig out of these sample numbers that have not yet been mentioned. There are still a few there.

THE DEVIL'S NUMBER 666

For years I have heard of what is described as the devil's number, and poor 6 has been the butt of the abuse for being that number. How can a number of reason and worry be the devil's number?

My own interpretation of this is simple. Nine is the number of spiritual development, and the reverse of this would be the so called devil's number. Therefore I consider that inverted 9 is the devil's number, which is the exact opposite of spiritual development. If there is a devil's number, then it would indicate un-development of spirit. Invert the 9 and it looks like a 6, but it is NOT a 6. An inverted 9 shall always be, and remain an inverted 9.

Of course any person with three 6s in their birth date would be a candidate for the psychiatrist's couch because they would be a worrier in the extreme, but that does not make them in league with the devil in any way. I have heard people accused of this because they had three 6s, but why would the Soul hand itself over to the devil. After all the Soul is under the control of the Monad, which is the close friend of God. Such a thing is for novelists and horror movie producers, and is in my opinion utter rubbish and should never be contemplated as fact for a moment.

SELF-AWARENESS

A very good lesson now is to do your own numerology. Read the number honestly without trying to stretch them to what you would like them to be. To do otherwise you are only deluding yourself and you will always know in your heart that such a dishonest reading is rubbish. You might be amazed at your good points, or you may be upset by your bad tendencies, but remember you have free will to have dominance over these traits. That is the point of your lessons in this life: to rise above and control your bad traits. Always be objective and scrupulously honest in these readings, for twisting them is then just a waste of time doing them in the first place. Remember these are just lessons, and I reiterate—we can always dominate our bad tendencies, but first we have to know what these tendencies are. For finding these tendencies, numerology is an unsurpassed tool.

Remember no one person is ever fully positive or negative. Without any pressure we can all be positive, but when stress and pressure is applied, we all tend to revert to our basic numerological personality unless we have learned to keep this in check.

Numerology can be a prized asset to the intelligent if used with wisdom, but it can also be used as a weapon to hurt by the ignorant, therefore don't join the ignorant fraternity. There are too many of those ignoramuses in the world already. Use numerology wisely for the good of humanity, for any attempt to hurt people with this will bring about more karma on yourself. Remember, "As you sow, so shall you reap."

Always point out the numerical advantages strongly as the last statement made, so that the personality you are reading for is left with the most positive note possible. Showing their most positive traits may help them dwell on these points and improve their demeanor to the point of self-improvement, but this will never happen if you leave the person with a grim picture of themselves.

If a person can tell you the time they were born, then it is almost a surety that if they were born in the early hours of the morning, they will be early risers throughout their lives and sharpest in these early AM hours. The same will apply for those born late at night, and they will usually be night owls and their thinking comes alive at late evening towards midnight.

While these trends have not been documented in the numerology texts, I have taken notice over the years and found that these tendencies to AM and PM sharpness of mind has always worked out as stated above. As I have been looking at this over a period of some twenty years, I do believe that this is a genuine trend of the personality.

Remember, practice is the key to good and rapid inter-pretation, and there is NO substitute for practice.

ABOUT THE AUTHOR

Archbishop Frank Bugge, D.D. has had a checkered career: electrician, motor mechanic, engineer, boiler construction and maintenance, engine driver, truck driver, fork lift driver, musician, security guard, and Archbishop.

As a child he could see and hear from the Spirit world and was always in trouble for "telling lies" about the spirits, so he soon learned to keep his mouth shut for fear of more reprisals.

He became a church organist in his teens and was very drawn to the church, but was not satisfied with the standard teachings within churches, and was always seeking answers. In the early 1970s, Archbishop Bugge encountered a Rev Father John King of the Liberal Catholic Church, who was also quite clairvoyant, and so found a kindred spirit. The Rev Father King taught the basics of pure numerology to him, and thus enlivened his curiosity in this direction. All his life, he has sought out other esoteric information and how it is affected and interpreted by numerology.

Archbishop Bugge gained more information from a Druid, Arch Mage (Tim Ryan), who was to further expand his knowledge in this subject. Over thirty-plus years, he has delved into other psychic realms, noting their relationship to the numbers, which has resulted in an even stronger grasp of the subject and better accuracy in the fine detail.

Throughout the years Archbishop Bugge has used numerology for counselling, and taught many professional counsellors this art, which has been used to great advantage by them.

During this time Archbishop Bugge has had the distinct honor and unique privilege to study directly with the Late Archbishop Herman Adrian Spruit, and Archbishop Mother Meri Spruit, Patriarch and Matriarch of the worldwide Catholic Apostolic Church of Antioch—Malabar Rite. During this time, the Archbishop took advantage of the opportunity to absorb the wisdom from both these wonderful people who gave of it so freely and with great love, and states, "To this day they remain my role models, whom I shall sadly never be able to match, for they led by high example beyond my capability, and not just words."

These two loving people resulted in strengthening Bugge's inspiration in becoming an Archbishop within the church himself. At the time of writing Frank Bugge is the presiding Archbishop of the Australian Branch of the Worldwide Catholic Apostolic Church of Antioch, located in Melbourne Australia, and can be contacted on email at archprime@yahoo.com.au

More Books from Blue Dolphin Publishing

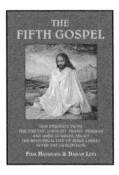

The Fifth Gospel
New Evidence from the Tibetan, Sanskrit, Arabic, Persian and Urdu Sources About the Historical Life of Jesus Christ After the Crucifixion
Fida Hassnain & Dahan Levi
ISBN: 978-1-57733-181-0, 344 pp., 6x9, paper, $19.95

Reincarnation for Christians
Evidence from Early Christian and Jewish Mystical Traditions
John W. Sweeley, Th.D.
ISBN: 978-1-57733-265-7, 294 pp., 6x9, paper, $22.00

Metaphysical Techniques That Really Work
Audrey Craft Davis
ISBN: 978-1-57733-128-5, 148 pp., 5.5 x 8.5, paper, $14.95

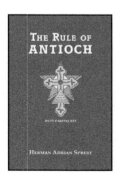

The Rule of Antioch
Herman Adrian Spruit
ISBN: 978-1-57733-255-8, 66 pp., 5.5 x 8.5, paper, $10.00

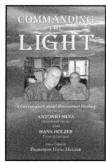

Consciousness Is All
Now Life Is Completely New
Peter Francis Dziuban
ISBN: 978-1-57733-160-5, 340 pp., 6 x 9,
paper, $22.00

Esoteric Healing
*A Practical Guide Based on
the Teachings of the Tibetan in the
Works of Alice A. Bailey*
Alan Hopking
ISBN: 978-1-57733-110-0, 384 pp., 6x9,
paper, $25.00

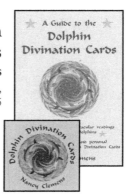

Commanding the Light
*A Conversation About Paranormal
Healing Between Antonio Silva,
Paranormal Healer, and Hans Holzer,
Parapsychologist*
Antonio Silva and Hans Holzer
ISBN: 978-1-57733-213-8, 116 pp., 5 x 8,
paper, $13.00

A Guide to the Dolphin Divination Cards
Nancy Clemens
ISBN: 978-1-57733-017-2, 388 pp., 6x9,
paper, $19.95

Dolphin Divination Cards
Nancy Clemens
ISBN: 978-0-931892-79-0, 108 round
cards, boxed, $13.00

Printed in Great Britain
by Amazon

41529969R00071